FIND_.._ SPIRITUAL FREEDOM
THROUGH THE STORIES OF THE BIBLE

Gift from
Gerald Epstein
to
Hannelore Hahn

Climbing Jacob's Ladder

Finding Spiritual Freedom through the Stories of the Bible

by

Gerald Epstein, M.D.

ACMI PRESS
NEW YORK

ISBN: 1-883148-07-3
Library of Congress Cataloging-in-publication data available

First Edition Published 1999 by
ACMI PRESS
351 East 84th Street
New York, NY 10028

Designed by
STUDIO 31, INC.

Printed in the U.S.A.

Table of Contents

Preface

When I trained in psychiatry and psychoanalysis, it was axiomatic in these fields that the aim for each of us was to find liberation or freedom, and psychoanalysis promised us the way to find it.

What has continued to reverberate within me is the truth that we all seek liberation. Eventually I recognized that a non-spiritually-based system like psychoanalysis could not really fulfill that aim, but only through the life of spirit could such freedom be attained. For it is one of our givens at birth, a possibility that inheres in being born, which has been forgotten. In order to realize that possibility, we have to take responsibility to search for that elusive freedom, open ourselves to a new way of looking at reality, and diligently practice reversing our habitual modes of behaving and thinking. In return we are rewarded with experiencing the genuine inner-generated hope and unprejudiced attitude to life that one needs to live fully in the world.

My spiritual awakening began in 1974, when I was visiting Jerusalem. At that time I was a practicing Freudian psychoanalyst and a trained medical doctor. At thirty-eight I was confident that I had found the "royal" road to personal freedom, but doubts were creeping in because of the time and money clients poured into the process without much to show for it.

In Jerusalem I met a young man who had undergone extensive psychoanalysis to rid himself of persistent depression. After a fruitless three years in therapy, he met a woman who practiced "visual imagery." He had met with her four times within a month and now considered himself cured.

Given my training, I could hardly believe him. Yet the fact remained that in one month, with a new and different therapy, his depression had lifted.

My interest aroused, I met with his therapist, Mme. Colette Aboulker-Muscat. That meeting changed my life. In that encounter, which I described in *Healing Visualizations* (New York: Bantam, 1989), I discovered the way to gain freedom in this life. This is what I imparting in the book.

I apprenticed with Madame Muscat for nine years. During my training I learned that each person's mission is to climb what Colette has termed "the ladder of self-mastery" that brings mind and body together in preparation for eventually making union with God. In fact, this divine union is the esoteric mission of all Western people adhering to the three great monotheistic faiths of Judaism, Christianity, and Islam. It is the way of the unity of two becoming one. It is a path of love with the union of a beloved (God) and the lover (us). What I discovered in my journey to freedom — that is by no means completed — is that it can only be found by relinquishing our attachments to anything in life taking us away from the Divine. Thus, freedom and God are inextricably interwoven.

As I discovered in my own journey, the path of self-mastery requires inner and outer practices, an intention to climb the ladder no matter what the cost, and a constant state of vigilance the practice necessitates. I liken these practices to the rungs of a ladder, in that they must be climbed one by one till we reach the top of ourselves.

The outer practices are the Ten Commandments. They represent the laws we use to relate to each other to create harmony and to how communities may work together in mutual cooperation. The inner practices are known as the three intentions—surrendering our ego, living moderately, and practicing faithfulness in our relationships. Whether a tradition states them explicitly as Christianity does as the Three Vows of Obedience, Poverty, and Chastity—or implicitly, as they are present in every tradition, for without them it is virtually impossible to detach from the deceptions imposed upon us by the manmade world. These deceits, illusions, or false beliefs, however you may like to call them, are like sticky flypaper. They are hard to shake off, but can be done so with determination.

These inner intentions are intimately related to the outer ones. Together they constitute what may be termed "mystical ethics," a term first coined about four centuries ago by a mystical sage in Israel named Moses Cordevero.

In my own odyssey I came to recognize that the inner and outer are an interactive system. Without one being operative, the other either becomes unavailable, or mechanical as a practice.

In the spiritual tradition of the West, the commandments and the vows were first conveyed through the Bible. It describes the moral history of the world in the form of stories about real-life people living real-life events to which we could all immediately relate. What happened to those biblical figures was not really different from what has happened and does happen to you and me in the course of our social relationships that form the fabric and substance of life. The fabric and substance the Bible expresses are: responsibility, relationship, and community life. They are all part of the moral fabric that is the unique Hebraic contribution to world spirituality. It is from this moral perspective that spiritual freedom can become a lived possibility. And, so it is that these Bible stories can be read on a moral level. As well, they can be read on a literal/historical, analogical or allegorical, moral and secret/esoteric/spiritual level.

In this book I explore some biblical stories on these four levels and interweave the presence of the commandments and vows in them to show how they participate in the lives of these biblical personages, and by extension, us as well.

I do not presume to provide an exhaustive application of

these stories, but rather hope to give a taste of the deep wisdom embedded in this book to serve as a springboard to catapult us forward to liberation.

As a unique contribution I have translated each of the Bible stories into a series of mental imagery exercises where we shall be able to emotionally and intuitively connect to their heroes, heroines, and antiheroes, and discover new meaning and possibilities for our personal lives.

Mental imagery is the revelatory language that connects us to invisible reality. The imagery process gives us instant understanding of inner life and gives us a direct access to truth. It bypasses our habitual mode of logical thought, which itself is not the proper vehicle to glean inner truth, nor to take us to freedom. The intuitive process, of which imagery is a major form, draws us to truth, while logical thought helps us to navigate through our physical excursion in everyday life. It helps us carry out the truths gleaned through intuitive processes.

CHAPTER ONE

LADDER OF SELF-MASTERY

The story of creation in one Jewish mystical tradition of the West says that when God poured light into the worlds of creation, the vessels that were created to contain His light couldn't do so and they broke. These fragments descended through the upper reaches of creation to the lower realms, which were in darkness. Some light escaped from these vessels and remained in the upper realms. However, some sparks clung to the inner surface of these shards and were trapped by these pieces. God needed to retrieve this imprisoned light and sent emissaries to the lower realm — known as Earth — to recover and liberate those sparks. The emissaries were/are called human beings.

So, we are here to retrieve something very precious. This is our hero's journey. The road is fraught with danger because we can and do make errors along the way and forget our mission. Nevertheless, God said this creation is "good" (Gen. 1), and we are always put to the test to remember that. In remembering our true nature of being in God's image and likeness, we are actually recapturing the light. We are simultaneously healing ourselves, healing the world, and restoring light to God.

Becoming heroic is shedding the world of darkness, ascending the ladder of self-mastery, and initiating our identification with Spirit to eventually make union.

The knowledge of Spirit has been with us since the beginning of human existence. The turn to Spirit has called many, in fact, but few have been able to weather the forces of the serpent, who distracted Eve in Eden (see p. 38 below), that have sought to deter us from making that climb to freedom. Most of us to date have accepted our trapped condition, finding our will to free ourselves sapped by all the diversions placed in our path, viz., drugs, alcohol, uncontrolled sexual activity, craving for money and fame, and illness, to name a few. We have focused our understanding of heroism essentially on the physical plane, as it has been fed to us through heroic acts in incessant wars, and reiterated in comic book "heroes" to movie "heroes" of the ilk of John Wayne.

Heroics on the physical level pale by comparison to what it takes on the inner level. What has to be overcome here is the resistances of: inertia, habit, outer threats, intimidation, and sensory gratification. What awaits us at the end of the ascent is true freedom, unlimited joy.

CHAPTER TWO

ROADBLOCKS TO FREEDOM:
UNCOVERING THE TERRORISTS

The great paradox of our human existence is that while we yearn for and strive after freedom, in whatever way each of us may seek to define that word, we find that we are no closer to that elusive element than were our ancestors. We are in captivity either physically, mentally, emotionally, or socially in ways far more exquisite than our forebears could ever have dreamed. It is incredible that over 75 percent of the human race is in some sort of captivity from which they can never escape. The world has become a place of bondage of one sort or another for almost every one of us.

The great Islamic mystic poet J'Alladin Rumi said that this world is comprised of thieves, drunkards, and murderers.[1] This sentiment, coming from a sage who wrote some of the most beautiful love poetry ever known, was written about eight hundred years ago. Nothing much has changed during the ensuing millennium (nor was it much different for the preceding four millennia). The basic instinct of a male-dominated world is to murder, steal, commit adultery, and appropriate what isn't theirs. All of the great Western religions have sought to thwart, control, or otherwise channel these urges without much success. I say "religions" in their exoteric or worldly teaching. The exoteric, or rational focus, devoid of the esoteric, or intuitive foundation, have been unsuccessful in their efforts to tame the bestiality that besieges the world. What is missing from these teachings has been the deeper meanings that carry the weight of truth that institutionalized religious teachings have failed to convey.

It now becomes more urgent for the need to replace these institutional forms with teachings and practices derived from esoteric or spiritual sources, which are directly arrayed against institutionalization of any kind, and their consequent urge to gain power over others, which is a *natural* outgrowth of any organization. The necessity for this change is more pressing now because we are more directly in charge, than ever before, of controlling the course of the continued existence or destruction of the planet.

Even these individuals and institutions thirsting for power and domination are seeking freedom. They are doing so believing it will come through the subjugation of others to their will. The urge for freedom is an inherent impulse, much like the inner urges of sex and aggression described by Freud, and the need to worship described by me later on.

We can find this impulse being expressed in so many of our everyday actions, but expressed in a distorted and sometimes perverse way. For instance, the taking of drugs and alcohol are really attempts, at base, to find a way out of the constriction, enslavement, and bondage felt by so much of the world's population. I think this fact has been overlooked in the moralizing posturing of those of us passing judgment on drug addicts and alcoholics. The destructiveness created by those people makes them accountable. However, to "declare war" on them serves to further a misconception that those fellow humans are different from us in kind rather than in degree. It should be understood that all of us are rowing *in the same boat* in this world. The drug and alcohol addicts are exaggerations of our tendencies. In fact, we all share basic themes that make up the lived experience of the human race, although they are uniquely lived out in our individual stories concerning them.

Even hysteria and suicide, as extreme examples, are instances of attempts to gain freedom, albeit in a distorted and eventually injurious manner. The person who is acting in a schizophrenic way is but an extreme example of our own tendencies. By labeling him we automatically relegate him to another world, alien and removed from ours. The psychiatrist who quickly condemns this tortured individual's soul by pronouncing him insane in this way is actually saying: "Whew! That's not me. He is different in kind from me." In this way we don't have to look at reflections of our own behavior.

In sum: each of us is looking for our release from our shackles. Accordingly, we exercise whatever options seem available to us at the time.

That we are free is contained in the very fact of our birth. In the esoteric literature, God created the world through a "divine contraction": As All Infinite Being covered everything, everywhere, the Creator dreamt of human existence. Following His dream He proceeded to fulfill it by withdrawing into Himself. In doing so a void was created out of which emanated the created world. This void we consider to be a space of freedom from which everything is permitted to emerge. The microcosmic version of this event is our individual birth. We emerge from the void created in the womb, and with the aid of uterine contractions we make our way into the world completely free. By coming into this world we become part of the great chain of being that begins with God and descends down the ladder of concrete beings, albeit invisible to our ordinary perceptions, starting with seraphim to cherubim, thrones, dominions, virtues, powers, principalities, archangels, angels, and finally humans, the final link in the chain. Every being in this hierarchy of being exists, and is free by virtue of that creation/existence.

To be truly free is to be immortal. Every being created in this great chain is inherently immortal. All the beings above us in the chain know they are in eternal life, the life of God. We are the only beings who do not know this and have sacrificed this knowledge by choosing to remain mortal, i.e., to die.

Therefore, being born is the monumental act of freedom to which each of us is exposed, and then we surrender it through the errors in living we commit from very early life onwards. In our very existence we have access to the *phenomenal* world — the world of experience — and the *noumenal* world of inner revelation, intuitive knowledge, and the love.

What are the basic errors? There are two: wanting to be God, and giving away our own authority of what we know to be true. I speak of the former in the next chapter. For now I'll concentrate on the latter.

We give away our authority when we surrender to the institutions that govern the world and to the inner allies of these institutions called "false selves." Just like the serpent in the garden lied to Eve, so these outer and inner terrorists inculcate false beliefs and values about life that are fundamentally preposterous.

In the mystical system of the West these battles between the terrorists and our true self, or nature, are described as the battle between the forces of light versus darkness, or in more religiously tinged vernacular, good vs. evil.

The institutions I speak of are: theological, political/military, medical (including psychology), corporate (big business), scientific. Each institution sets standards of behavior and beliefs that we are intimidated, seduced, or hypnotized into accepting as true. Theological institutions — organized religions — set the ideal of who is good and who is bad. The political/military set the standard of who is friend and who is foe. The medical institutions set standards of who is normal (healthy) and who is abnormal. Business sets the standard of what's in and what's out. Science sets standards for what is real and what is not real. The media and educational institutions reinforce these ideologies.

Each standard involves some elements of competition requiring us to compare ourselves to one another and to ourselves. We are constantly involved in critical value judgments of good-bad, right-wrong in some variant or other of these two. To set ourselves up in such a capacity makes us stand as an arbiter of another person's reality, effectively putting us in the position of playing God, as though we have the capacity to make such assessments. This applies equally to our tendency to judge ourselves as though these standards have any merit, value, or validity for our lives.

At base these institutions want to maintain their power and suppress any truth that will undermine their control. They maintain such control by constantly suggesting that things are terrible (i.e., not up to standard) and only by following their authority can we gain any measure of security.

Further, they seek to block any direct experience of truth we have by labeling it heretical (theological), unpatriotic (political/military), charlatanism (medical), or antiquated (corporate). Hypnotizing us into believing they are the "highest" authorities, we are cut off from our own inner truth regarding our inherent connectedness to each other, to nature, and to God. This inherent connectedness was described by Professor Morris Berman, in his book *The Reenchantment of the World,* as "participating consciousness." Institutions achieve this power by taking advantage of our natural, inborn impulse to worship; to search for models for us to venerate and adore. In diverting our attention away from our direct connection to the divine, the institutions admonish us to follow the herd and be "good," support war and political philandering, buy Windows 95, the list goes on.

We are indoctrinated to believe that natural science holds the answer to solving the ills of life; political avenues can solve the social ills of our world; and that current medical practice can really prevent and cure illness (note that every epidemic illness supposedly eradicated by vaccines and antibiotics is back). These beliefs are reinforced and ingrained in most of us in our early schooling. However,

OUR FREEDOM CAN NEVER COME
THROUGH THE AGENCY OF ANY INSTITUTION
CREATED BY THE HAND OF MAN.

As for the media, TV has, for the most part, made us into "spectators," not "participators," separating us from experiencing the natural world and our own creativity.

Over the centuries, we have permitted these institutions to subjugate and enslave us, by believing the nonsense doled out to us by them. We have even ardently sought to join forces with them to secure a piece of the power pie temptingly offered. On the face of it, it seems that these institutions are providing a safety net of security for so many of us either by coaxing us to join forces with them, or by our aligning ourselves with their value systems, that we are not aware of the mirage they create, or of the mirage we create for ourselves about what is necessary, important, and true about this life. By hooking into the mirages, we functionally keep ourselves in a state of torpor, a vegetative state of self-hypnosis, which prevails in the world now.

Paradoxically, as the world is becoming smaller through the means of telecommunications, and the ease of travel, we are getting a less distorted picture of what is going on in the world. We are now able to see by the evidence of our own senses the pain and suffering going on everywhere: Rwanda, Bosnia, Tibet, amongst others. Consequently, we are beginning to wake up to the atrocities happening everywhere, and to ourselves. With this awakening — an unintended byproduct of the technological age — comes the real possibility for freedom. We can achieve real liberation from the tyranny of all those institutions, and from the tyranny of these inner terrorists, those agents of the institutions, which we call the "false selves" (this wonderful denotation plus the nature of institutions was brought to my attention through the teaching of the late Dr. Bob Gibson, a true teacher of spiritual free-dom). These false selves want us dead and act as parasites of our being, draining us of our life force and keeping us asleep. They are in mortal combat with our true self, that aspect of our being that is the witness or observer who does not accept the lies of the false selves, nor the false standards propagated by the manmade institutions. When it is awake, the true self is fully aware of the differences between what is true and what is false. It is that awareness that serves to keep us in attunement with God's truth. It is often lulled to sleep by the hypnotic influence of the false selves who are mounting a constant assault against it. They are constantly working to drain our energy by supporting the false belief systems to which I have alluded. Every time we act on a false belief, we are harming ourselves. The injuries are reflected in physical and/or emotional malaise, often accompanied by social difficulties. Once the errors are made we have to expend energy to make corrections, thus siphoning our life force. The natural pathway from here is aging, decaying, diseasing, dying. There is no other alternative. The false selves have triumphed again!

THE FALSE SELVES ARE THE MAIN OBSTACLES
BLOCKING OUR WAY UP THE LADDER TO GOD.

False selves is another way of saying "ego." They have insinuated themselves into our personalities during the course of our early childhood development as/like little Pinocchios, whose job it is to lie and hypnotize us into a state of sleep-walking and sleep-talking while we are awake doing our everyday activity.

These inner espionage agents are divided into two camps: the defiant and compliant. The former seek to control the world through intimidation and threats so as to get those around them to do their bidding. The latter group act by seduction and flattery to gain just what the defiant group seeks. Both groups are looking for power and pleasure, while avoiding pain, and are thoroughly dependent on the outer world to give it to them.

The defiant ones intimidate by complaining, blaming, and claiming to have rights that when scrutinized more closely are not rights at all, but are really privileges. Privileges refer to something that can be bestowed on you or taken from you by someone else. When you examine what you "have" in life, you will see that nearly 100 percent are privileges, which we have misidentified as rights. Becoming aware of this fact is a humbling experience. The compliant seduce and flatter us by trying to please, by doing what the authorities tell us is right for us (because the authorities supposedly know more about us than we do about ourselves), or by trying to be different, i.e., being unique to win some reward from the world. Simply listen to your inner dialogue, and you will hear yourself blaming others, complaining about one thing or another, or how unfairly you have been treated. Or, you'll inwardly hear how you have to please, or placate someone, look to someone else to tell you what to do, or how you have to change yourself to become special and be noticed. In our overall personality strategy we tend to align ourselves with being more compliant or more defiant.

Let me describe some characteristics of these false selves. They always speak in the future or past tense. The future hasn't happened, the past is finished. Neither exist now, and are thus false. This tendency makes them easily recognizable. There is no one who doesn't know those tenses when listening to the inner dialogue that is constantly going on, or is listening to the outer voices endlessly bombarding us. Refuse to support these voices. Have faith. Don't give in to them. They are all speaking untruths. Don't converse with them.

The false selves are quite clever. They appear to ally themselves with the True Self and be in agreement with your very good intentions. Take the example of the false self of a problem drinker: "You are perfectly right. My drinking has created a problem for everyone around me. I am definitely *going to stop* right away." Notice the good intention couched in the future tense. A clever false self just spoke to us. Don't believe him for a moment. That drinking is definitely not stopping.

There is no end to the vigilance required to root out false selves. It is a full-time job, maybe the most important job we are given on earth. It is not a thankless job, even though there is no vacation time, no retirement benefits. It is actually the most rewarding job we can assume. For to put false selves (which include institutions) to rout places us squarely on the path to God. To be vigilant is not to become a vigilante. Don't think of this process as going into battle. We are merely declaring truth, not war.

One of the most insidious activities of false selves is their tendency to proclaim their rights. Standing up for rights in an American institution. We are, perhaps, one of the few places on earth were injustices can be corrected by social action on a regular basis; witness the governmental response to anti-war protests during the Vietnam War era. Wrongs can, and certainly need to be, righted. In the main, though, most clamoring after personal, as opposed to political, "rights" is a false self speaking. The overwhelming majority of rights that we think we deserve are in fact privileges.

Over the years I have seen this error played out innumerable times as patients lamented how they were not loved as children, holding on to this complaint in adult life to justify the present emotional pain they are suffering. They were supported in those complaints by a point of view in psychology that would tend to lay blame for our troubles in early childhood and corroborate the *right* to be loved as a child by one's parents. To be loved in childhood is a privilege, not a right, simply because it can be given or taken away by the parent(s). I suggest that we begin taking stock of what are really our inalienable rights earned by our merit and irremovable versus what are privileges. We may discover that we have the right to weed out the inner and outer terrorists. Seeing how we are mistaking privileges for rights is one of the great humbling experiences, which makes us also realize just how life is sacred.

We can reduce false-self behavior to one fundamental theme: wanting everything our own way. This attitude is ego-centered and self-serving, and has the effect of draining our energy. It isn't surprising, though, since all errors in living involve enormous energy waste and depletion; while living in attunement with the laws of Spirit is energy conserving and energizing.

Wanting our own way is lived out in the world by our false needs to be important, get approval, gain acceptance, get attention, and have pleasure without pain. They are false because they are manmade standards. We will do *anything* in the world to satisfy these urges, and in doing so will violate every commandment. The commandments are indeed a hedge and a protection against these urges. The satisfaction of these urges is at the behest of the will to power and is at the expense of our integrity and freedom. Each of them requires that we be a slave, since the satisfaction of them makes us utterly dependent on the outside world, i.e., others, for their fulfillment.

The false self's existence is entirely dependent on receiving some attention or reward from the outer world. Such living in a dependent mode makes it virtually impossible to become autonomously self-authoritative. As we shall see in the next chapter, to follow the Second Commandment and become our own authority is a necessary rung on the ladder to God. The pressures on us to abdicate self-authority are tremendous. Within the stream of ordinary societal life and the herd mentality, the messages support our depending on, listening to, and obeying outer authorities.

Without becoming self-authorities, there is no chance for becoming free. This assertion cannot be repeated often enough, because we will readily forget if we are not constantly reminded. The forces of darkness operate by hypnotic suggestion to make us forget who we really are and why we are really here.

I have been struck in my own experience just how frightened most everyone is of discovering and living freely. When that door has opened to reveal that light, I have seen so many people recoil and retreat to the familiarity of the accustomed, habitually enslaved life. In my clinical practice, I have noticed that some individuals would say they felt like they were in prison. In our imaginal work I took that as a cue to offer them the opportunity to leave this prison via a mental imagery exercise where they imagined themselves in a cell. They would search for the key, find it, and open the door, then go out and explore their surroundings. Interestingly, they would find the key, open the door, but *would not* leave.

I was puzzled by this phenomenon until one day a then-student and now friend of mine named Judy Besserman said she had been doing this exercise with patients and said to them to take the key with them when leaving the cell, *knowing they could return whenever they wished,* whereupon they would invariably go. I tried this in my practice and it worked! Enslavement has to always exist as a possibility to entertain should freedom prove too frightening.

The inner terrorists are our greatest challenge, making us more afraid than can any outer enemy. The fundamental aim of spiritual practice is to battle fears and anxieties arising from the inner realms of consciousness. When we take care of the inner terrorists, the outer world takes care of itself for us. Our emphasis is to control the inner circumstances, not the outer ones. Don't believe for one moment that controlling external matters would relieve us of our inner tensions, a propaganda story fed to us for millennia.

Now that we have looked at the terrorists, how might we begin to define freedom? One definition of freedom might be: the absence of being defined in life by what we do or have. It is being alive to the present moment without making up stories about the future or the past, and being able in that context to perceive the facts of the circumstances you encounter. Freedom means being able to stand up to the inner terrorists that paralyze our actions and force us to march along with/in the herd mentality. It means not being open to suggestion and freeing ourselves from the hypnotic spell created by the institutions that govern our lives.

A truly free person might be defined as one who is not caught up in having vanity or pride. He/she is detached and selfless at the same time, participating in the welfare of others, while not sacrificing him/herself on the altar of other people's ego-centered needs. S/he is nobody's master and is nobody's slave. S/he is the master of him/herself.

It seems that free persons pursue fulfillment through love, not power. Is there an essential difference between the one who seeks the path of power and the one who seeks the path of law and love? Do they have anything in common? The answer to both question is "yes." Both are seeking freedom — as we all want liberation. The person on the path of power, however, is seeking it in a dependent, hopelessly enslaved way. Even a king is dependent on his vassals to extol and revere him. In power relationships, there is always a mutual dependency established which has the effect of curtailing our individual freedom.

The person on the path to God becomes autonomous and develops mutually interdependent relationships existing in a community of like-minded people, all of whom are searching for authentic meaning to/in life.

It is in the manner of searching — through power or through love — that the essential difference lies between the thief, drunkard, murderer on the one hand, and the moderate, chaste, obedient soul on the other. The latter's life is not counterfeit, in that it is not predicated on what anyone else has to furnish it. There are no contingent dependencies, no conditions that have to be met to bring it to fulfillment. It is this unconditional state that is the basis of true love, the only authentic love there is. Truth and authenticity are synonymous.

In the dependent behaviors I have mentioned, love is absent. Without love, life does not perpetuate itself in a constructive manner, for it is only by giving instead of getting can the force of love overcome the force of death, a possibility stated by King Solomon nearly three thousand years ago when he said in Song of Songs (8:6) "Love is strong as death."

What are the ways we can use to free ourselves from these terrorists? Let's turn to the practices of the Three Vows and Ten Commandments for help in answering this question.

CHAPTER THREE

LAW AND ORDER

The singular contribution of the Western spiritual approach is that the healing of our fragmented self lies within the context of our social/communal relationships. This means that the particular difficulties besetting us are wedded to a larger social matrix or buildup out of which all illness springs. Social matrix translates into social relationships. We are all fundamentally social beings. It is the essence of living on Earth. We can choose to be close to or distant from others, loving or hateful toward others, but all of our decisions and actions are governed by the social network in which we live. The cement that holds relationships together in a cohesive, cooperative, and collaborative way is the Ten Commandments and the Three Vows. These cosmic prescriptions provide the "sounding board "against which we bounce off our interpersonal decisions. We are always either acting in concert with those precepts or acting in error with regard to them. Individual illness, family breakdown, marital dissolution, community deterioration, all represent an error in living, in attunement and connection to Spirit.

The Three Vows and Ten Commandments are two of the pivotal spiritual practices of Monotheism, the traditional spiritual path of the West. They require that we live in community and not retreat from our everyday world, for their practice creates the *necessity* of our usual life activity to engage in them.

The vows represent the inner attitudinal practice. Here we assume a new relationship to ourselves. We take on a new set of beliefs to replace those to which we have accepted as valuable. Operating from this different position makes it much easier to relate to others, and in making a contribution in the world. Regarding the former: we no longer need to exploit the other person since all the vows have to do with giving, not getting. By giving we apply that to our relationship to the world, where we feel impelled naturally, by implementing the vows, to share with others what we have to benefit them. In doing so we participate actively in helping to heal the world, a tenet that has always been at the heart of monotheism.

The Ten Commandments define our outer activity as we interact in relationship to others and to God. All that we do revolves around these relationships, in which we either create strife or serenity. We have been given the means to achieve the latter via the code of laws provided to Moses. Our job has been to live by this code, which is to dictate our behavior.

By integrating new attitudes and actions that are embodied in the Three Vows and the Ten Commandments, we can begin the repair of ourselves and our world. The underlying essence of these attitudinal changes begins with developing the spiritual practices of detachment and disidentification.

The Three Vows

Throughout the world's traditions devotees to a practice are asked to make three promises about conducting their relationship to life. The pledges are: to surrender one's sense of personal importance, relinquish the impulse to acquire, and to curb the urge toward indiscriminate sexual and other intoxicating activity. In monotheistic practice, especially in its Christian modification, these vows were explicitly stated as: obedience, poverty, and chastity, respectively. They represent the opposite tendencies of three highly destructive ones engaged in either singly or in combination by most of the world's population. These three are: tyranny, greed, debauchery.

Tyranny includes dictatorship, fascism, marauding, murder, and enslaving. Greed is the heart of thievery. It is defined as wanting more, better, and different, which leads to ceaseless acquisition and holding onto material possessions, even murdering to do so. Debauchery encompasses intoxications of all sorts. They are literal wells of destructive poison, cutting a swath of havoc throughout society (for instance, Alcoholics Anonymous has estimated that every alcoholic destroys the lives of seven people around them). All the vices are destructive by nature and are arrayed toward putting an end to life. The virtues are arrayed to be constructive and toward perpetuating life. They make us harmless (not tyrannical), contributing to life (not greedy), and considerate (not debauched).

Becoming free lies in the act of taking the three vows of obedience, poverty, and chastity. In contemporary terms we can call them respectively, "surrender," "moderation," and "faithfulness." It is an absolute first step without which freedom becomes inaccessible. You can seminar and workshop yourself endlessly; you can find loving relationships and walk over hot coals; you can take sesame oil baths and escape from fear. No matter what you do, what I have said is inescapable: without the vows everything you do is merely an avenue to finding another pleasurable experience that satisfies for a while only to be replaced by more mirages. It is not that these experiences are bad or unnecessary, but they cannot liberate you.

What does liberate us is the practice of the vows and commandments which teach us to detach and disidentify from our attachment to material life and material success. We are not to define who we are by what we have (detachment), or by what we do (disidentify). Materialism can be of the physical or mental variety. Mental materialism means being attached to thoughts and feelings. These thoughts can be of the inner verbal type and/or can be of an imagery sort, like fantasies or daydreams. Thoughts can be of the past or future, which are held onto as precious possessions. In all spiritual traditions, thoughts of this nature are viewed as impediments to spiritual attunement simply because such mentation characteristically lead us into blind alleys, or some other sort of impasse.

The Ten Commandments

What was conveyed to Abraham by God orally was passed on to Moses in the written form of the Ten Commandments. In between the Israelites became enslaved for four hundred years in the land of material attachment, and so forgot their basic commitment. They were reminded, this time etched in stone. This law of life was passed on to everyone while undergoing spiritual training in the desert. It was given here so it could be brought into the world of everyday human life as a guiding star for steering our course through life.

The first five commandments detail our relationship to God:

1. Don't put any god before God, or between you and God;
2. Don't make graven images, or erect idols before which you bow down;
3. Don't take God's name in vain;
4. Remember the Sabbath;
5. Honor your father and mother so you may live a long life.

The second five commandments refer to our relationship to each other:

6. Don't murder;
7. Don't commit adultery;

8. Don't steal;
9. Don't bear false witness;
10. Don't covet.

The Ten Commandments are our karmic safety net.[2] The continuance of life depends on living according to them, so as not to accrue a moral karmic debt for which the consequences may come back to haunt us in this life in the form of: illness, tragedy, personal suffering.

This law of payment even transcends our individual lifetime. As the Bible states that the "sins" (errors) of our fathers are passed down three to four generations. So, we may not see something affecting an individual through his/her life, but the offspring may be quite afflicted, as is often the case. Generally, when children are afflicted, parents don't look to the actions of their lives as having any contribution to what the child suffers, except in the case now of mothers who smoke, drink, or take drugs and are aware that these substances directly affect the baby's development. Nonetheless, the family errors are passed down via the psychogenetic as well as genetic inheritance. Psychogenetic transmission is analogous to physical genetic transmission. This transmission means the passing down of the non-physical traits, qualities, and tendencies of family dispositions through success generations. This passing down includes family social strengths and social errors. By our birth we always have the opportunity to correct the family error(s).

Every error we make in life has to do with misusing the commandments. In Eden, Eve and Adam took the decision to substitute knowledge received by revelation — the direct word of God — by knowledge received by experimentation, i.e., from the place of skepticism, of doubt.

* * *

The Ten Commandments and Three Vows are so important that I feel impelled to quote a passage from the anonymously written book *Meditations on the Tarot* (New York: Penguin Books), the classic work on the Western spiritual tradition. I have found it to summarize their relationship to the life of Spirit.

> The following are the essential conditions to which every viable spiritual tradition must adhere: it must be founded from above (direct revelation); it must observe the Ten Commandments and be inspired by the ideal of virginity (chastity); and its aim must be implied in the will which founded it (obedience), with every human programme [viz, agenda] withdrawn from it (poverty) (p. 296).

The Ten Commandments and the Three Vows for me are the most important guideposts to our existence on earth. There is no possible way to know what to do to live in clarity without such a set of beacons to light the way. To make these commandments and vows work for you, you have to obviously acquaint yourself with them so they are always in mind. They have to be memorized and repeated over and over again until they become etched in your mental sphere, so much so they are always on your mind, or are coming to mind. Doing so, you will find yourself forming a relationship with God. As you are accomplishing this task, and as an aid to accomplishing this task, you need to constantly ask yourself: what vow (or vows) commandment (or commandments) are at play in any given situation in which you find yourself.

Start to notice the many acts of gossip, dog-eat-dog behavior, stealing (i.e., not telling the waitress that you've been undercharged on the bill), character assassination, depressed behavior, cheating, envy, jealousy, wasting others' time (go to your doctor's appointment scheduled for 10 a.m. and not be seen until 12:30 p.m., taking over two hours of unpaid time from your paycheck, which the doctor doesn't give back to you), mixing in so many ways (a person came to me who conducted her business in the same room in which she was also doing her creative writing. I recommended she separate the two functions immediately).

Take a look at how you are feeling. If you are feeling angry or worried (and we can extend this to any other distressing feeling), you can be almost certain there is some error lurking with respect to these commandments. Anger usually relates to one of the three commandments: the Second Commandment, where anger relates to our feeling insulted or not being given our due importance. In other words, our ego-inflation has been pricked. Ego-inflation equals idolatry. Then there are angry murderous feelings that speak to the Sixth Commandment. Anger is a common response when we are competitive, jealous, or avaricious, all part of the Tenth Commandment.

When we worry, we are in the grip of making a graven image, a function of the Second Commandment. Why? Because when we worry we are squarely situated in the future. Yes, the feeling is genuine (as are all feelings), but it is the context that determines the value of the feeling. To draw conclusions, to construct stories about that illusory realm of the future, to speculate, all involve the mind engraving a fixed image just like we might do on a physical level. Once an image is carved, it is imbued with energy and has the capacity to draw our attention, interest, and even worship of it.

I could capture thousands of daily experiences to relate and tie them into the commandments. However, I leave this practice to you. I just wanted to give you a flavor of how the commandments are a hygienic practice for attaining mental — and physical — health, as well as a spiritual practice of awareness. As you begin seeing all of your behaviors within the context of the commandments, you will make errors. Make the corrections possible at the time. There is even making a correction concerning someone who has passed on. If this isn't feasible, promise yourself, in the present tense, not to make the error again. If you err again, no blame. Please do not criticize or condemn yourself for the error. Just proceed on to correct it, and don't make up a story about it. Remember, to forgive self is divine. Also, by behaviors I don't only mean physical. We include here too, mental activity, emotional states, verbal statements, gestures. There is nothing not subject to assessment within the purview of the commandments.

We can now find the application of the vows and commandments in the Bible stories, the subject of the next chapter.

CHAPTER FOUR

THE MORAL WAY: STORIES FROM THE BIBLE

All the biblical stories have messages embedded in them that speak to us on a number of levels: literal/historical, analogical/allegorical, aphoristic/moral, archetypal/spiritual. On a literal level they are to be taken as true events of the history of a people. The Bible is not a metaphorical work. When it says that Enoch and Elijah did not die, that is meant literally. The Red Sea parting is meant literally.

A careful reading of biblical stories provides answers to our questions and solutions to our problems. This is the analogical or allegorical way of understanding them. The analogical way is to show us the relationships between things, the way elements mirror each other, or reflect each other. Training ourselves to think by analogy gives us clarity in the moment and allows us to see the larger picture of something. When thinking analogically, we are thinking in wholes, and we can see how to direct our lives more beneficially and constructively. When Adam was in the Garden he named the animals. What he did was to assign form to qualities so that we could be reminded of the existence of these qualities and their possibility for fulfillment in an individual life. When Adam wanted to name courage he called it "lion"; in naming gentleness he called it "lamb"; in naming peacefulness he called it "dove"; and so on. The qualities and their physical representations are analogies of each other.

The aphoristic way means moral messages. The Ten Commandments are a moral message underscoring the necessity for restraint. When the commandments are breached, severe consequences befall the participants; when they are followed, beneficial consequences ensue.

On the archetypal or esoteric level, each of these figures bears a particular characteristic that exists in each of us, with whom we can readily identify. These qualities have to be cultivated to help us climb the ladder of self-mastery, or have to be rooted out else it would prevent our ascent. Every story has to be treated as a dream in that, like Western spiritual dream reading, every character and event represents a quality of us initially. We start by looking at what of ourselves is reflected or mirrored in the character or the situation. Thus, Cain, Abel, Goliath, David, etc., all represent inner aspects.

The spiritual dimension defines how we are to live our relationship between God and us. When we search for truth, we seek to live in the presence of the present, to live in no-time. When we look for freedom, we expand our spatial universe and by turning our focus to the vertical dimension of limitless spatiality, rather than look only to the horizontal dimension where our gaze is limited.

In sum: historical reality tells us what is happening in the world now. Moral reality tells us the way to live correctly in the world. Analogical reality tells us how to connect our relationship to time and how to live our time correctly. Spiritual reality tells us how to find God, which is the ultimate freedom.

Each bible story is complete in and of itself. That is to say, the unfolding of one story on the four levels and interweaving the role of the commandments and vows gives the knowledge that doing so for any other of the stories would evidence, with some slight variations. In this way the structure of the Bible is holographic, one element containing the whole. It seems to me the sages who redacted the Bible over the centuries wanted to impress their points by repetition, an excellent way to imprint knowledge. The various stories also keep our interest as we find the story unfolding from the creation of the world in Genesis to the closing of the Bible with II Chronicles, where each of us is exhorted to ascend to God as the final piece of advice. Between these two events is contained all the information any of us would ever need to pursue a life of freedom that never ends, that redeems and saves us, and allows us to restore Eden to ourselves.

EDEN: THE SETTING OF FREEDOM

The Garden of Eden represents the world of many possibilities and realities. There was once such a paradise on earth that remains as a collective memory in Western civilization, prompting us to yearn to regain that paradisaical place. Eden doesn't only exist as a physical locale, but also represents a place of peace, serenity, and happiness for us to recapture inwardly as a state of mind. It is a harmonization of body, mind, and spirit as we bring this trinity into unity. In this higher consciousness of existence, despair, disease, death, and all the excruciating pain of suffering is transcended, and the joy of truth and truth of joy is experienced.

It is the realm of absolute moral virtue that transcends the standards of right-wrong, good-bad set up by the institutions governing our life. In this transcendent space we are free, unfettered by living up to specious ideals. Eden is that place of utter freedom which is ours to enjoy for eternity. It is the transcendent reality that brings duality into unity, while being beyond that cohesion. Bringing duality into unity is a significant step on our climb of the ladder of self-mastery to find God. This is the search for which we have all been sent here to do by God, and which is the only reason for coming to inhabit this planet.

As Eden was a lived reality, so shall it become again a living reality for us. It is my belief that our world shall achieve the Edenic existence, which shall come through the efforts of we whom were created in the image and likeness of God, rather than through God Himself. At first God establishes the original Eden during the seven days of creation. We have to know that our creation is good just as God did during the days leading up to the creation of human life on the sixth day. Then we can come to know ourselves as "very good," as God knew us on the sixth day (Genesis 1:31).

That all the creation prior to our advent is very good means that there was never a question about the moral goodness of us, minerals, plants, animals, and all other species. However, besides humans, all the rest have no choice, no free will. When it comes to our creation, we have the choice of going beyond, of reaching a higher plane of existence, of bringing ourselves to the immortal plane of eternal life where we pass beyond the cycles of coming into being and passing out of being individually.

All the creation is magnificently beautiful, that beauty being constantly reproduced in each successive cycle of the coming and going of all that is above — stars, planets — and below here on earth.

Everything in creation follows God's law, the law of Truth. Everything, that is, except us. We are free not to follow that law even to the point of deceiving ourselves into believing that we can author our own laws that would somehow assume more credibility and validity than God's law. The fact of this freedom with which we are endowed by virtue of being born has led to our clouding of mind, and its faculties of perception, so that we are unable to apprehend the Eden that is here right now. Were we to wake up and clear away the cobwebs of confusion, we would be perceiving Eden right here at this very moment. This means that Eden is always here to anyone who takes the opportunity to make the discovery. The fall from Eden was to place a veil over our eyes so that we do not see through the illusion of contrived pseudo-events and fabricated stories that comprise our manmade creation. We are constantly elaborating stories to ourselves and to each other about things that don't exist, either focusing on the past or on the future; or the silly behavior we seriously undertake to fulfill some nonsensical standard that either someone else set up for us, or that we constructed for ourselves.

If we stop running into the past and future in our thoughts, stay in the moment, and decline the invitations to be good or bad, right or wrong, success or failure, normal or abnormal, or any one of the myriad sets of contrasting pairs seeking to compare us to each other and seeking to define us in terms of these invalid comparisons, then Eden immediately would appear to us.

First, though, we *have* to acknowledge that the man-made world does/cannot provide us with the happiness, fulfillment, and meaning for which we yearn. There is little argument there. People everywhere are bored with a strictly materially oriented life that has not succeeded (nor will it ever) in bringing the happiness we are looking for. We are so bored that we have to keep finding exquisitely more elaborate and exotic toys to stimulate us, keep us interested for a few nanoseconds. Then, we feel ourselves becoming desperate to find a new source of stimulation and gratification, if not on this planet, then off this planet. We will spend billions not feeding our starving brethren here on earth, but instead seek to land a manned mission on Mars. We do so because we either think that planet is populated, or we are looking for a place to escape to since we are destroying this planet. In either case, we have neglected to solve our problems on earth, and no off-planet escapade is going to bring us any closer to solving what must be taken care of first on earth. We are always looking for the solutions outside of rather than inside of ourselves. We need to explore inner space as a first priority before we could ever consider going to outer space.

Our leaders are so misguided and uninformed about the life of spirit that they continuously lead everyone astray and the herd continues to put up with it; the "it" referring to the mishandling of resources that ends up with a very few profiting at the expense of the overwhelming many, and making us all believe that it is unpatriotic to think or say otherwise. The times of the prophets haven't changed much from ancient days because the same garbage is being handed us as it has always been. The serpent never stops chattering, and we never stop believing him.

Do you really think for one moment that the institutions running this world could ever solve the problems for which they are the creators? It is these very institutions that have created the false standards that have no validity and yet have almost everyone running around trying to achieve.

It is this running around to be successful and avoid failure that dominates American life and keeps everyone from discovering Eden. Paradise has absolutely nothing to do with becoming successful. In fact, it has to do with giving up the desire for success. Becoming successful never succeeds in establishing the Eden we are seeking. Indeed, success has the effect of taking us further away into exile from happiness and contentment, unless the success we have acquired has to do with finding God, which we do by giving up the standard of success. Don't measure your success by any known material standard. Rather, absent yourself from judging yourself either a success or a failure or by any standard of perfection. Don't compare yourself to anyone or anything. You are your own measure. By doing so you are following the Tenth Commandment not to covet. Every standard invented by us humans has to do with coveting.

Instead of getting locked into the standards game, our job is to transcend the game — to not eat of the tree of knowledge of standards, which is what the manmade world is all about. We gain absolutely nothing in comparing ourselves to others unless we are interested in gaining an advantage over the next person, or in elevating ourselves to a status of supreme importance. Being covetous like this keeps us wholly dependent on those whom we are exploiting, for their existence actually is necessary to validate ours. That's the way it works in the world of unfreedom, which is the hallmark of the manmade world.

Eden is the world of freedom, of independence from the contingent dependencies that make up the relationship experience in the unfree world. A contingent dependency means: the validity of my experience, nay my very existence *depends* on your validating such experience or existence. That I exist is contingent on your acknowledgment of that. That's a contingent dependency. To be free requires no contingency. I am free whether you acknowledge it or not. To become this freedom is Eden. It is only possible by going inside, going to yourself and accepting to live by the Three Vows and Ten Commandments. There is no other way on earth to become free within the context of accepting to live in the community of (wo)mankind, loving one another in the framework of universal law, basking in the influx of divine love, seeking to work in concert with each other to heal the world — to change manslaughter to man's laughter.

To summarize simply: jump out of the standards trap we jump into Eden. Jump into the standards trap remain enslaved and forgo the opportunity of Eden.

ADAM AND EVE: FROM FREEDOM TO SLAVERY

Adam and Eve depict the search for spiritual transcendence in the coming together of our male and female energy, and the pitfalls therein. They are living in a paradisaical existence called Eden, which is a sheltered environment lying within the precincts of God the omniscient, omnipresent, omnipotent, All-Infinite Being who provides an atmosphere of never-ending bounty, eternal life, freedom, and truth. It is an otherworldly existence that is yet genuine, authentic, and possible for everyone to attain. Adam and Eve are Everyman and Everywoman.

The Bible conveys at once the past, present, and future of human existence in the same narrative. Adam and Eve in the Garden represent our human condition in which we have the Edenic paradise in our very grasp, yet let it slip away by engaging in the fundamental error that characterizes the plight of Western people: the desire to use the knowledge and power of God, to become God. This is what the serpent promised the couple in Eden by inveigling Eve to explore the realm of knowledge that was forbidden — the future — whereby they could *usurp* the knowledge and power of God. Everything that Western culture has stood for represents the eternal struggle between the forces of good and evil; good represents God, and evil represents the mistaken attempt of the human being to attain to that status.

The urge to usurpation is directly linked to the first of the Ten Commandments, namely, not to put any god before God, i.e., don't make the mistake of identifying the physical human being as the all-infinite Being. In spite of this admonition, the history of the Western world has been the endless recording of individuals trying to assert themselves as usurpers to the throne of God, with the result being endless wars, bloodshed, murder, and mayhem with crazed individuals leading their countries and countrymen to the slaughterhouse. At the time of this writing, there are currently seventy-five wars happening throughout the world.

The history of Western civilization portrays the dismal failure of our forefathers to pass the moral test set before us by God. For, what is the serpent's appearance in Eden other than the test sent by God to the young couple to test their resolve to walk in God's way by testing their moral uprightness and purity? You see, God's world is a morally perfect one. It is one created in truth, goodness, love, beauty, and freedom.

Given the possibility to experience Eden, why would we choose to die? We really want to live eternally and have freedom, so our attempt to usurp God's knowledge and power is done in ignorance of recognizing the unintended consequences of our actions. The mistake is not a malicious nor cunning one. We have been misled by belief systems that appear very attractive, tempting, and flattering. Promises are made, and, hypnotized as we are for most of our lives in waking consciousness, we succumb to the suggestions and propositions offered us. When we are open to suggestion we become a hypnotized person, and are ready to become enslaved to someone else's will.

I suspect, though, that Eve entertained the belief that she could become God, as is true for all of us, otherwise the serpent would not have had such a receptive audience for his proposition. What he showed Eve was the *way* to achieve fulfillment for this belief. What prompts that desire? I believe it comes from the free will and choice that we have all been granted as a birthright and prize for being born on the earth. By analogy, Eve and Adam were also possessed of a similar birthright. Being in a high moral plane — higher than we humans — Eve wanted, with an ardor hard for us to fathom, union with the magnificent heavenly Father. She *wanted to marry God*. The serpent promised her the marriage would happen if she ate the fruit. She misunderstood. She thought that becoming God would be tantamount to marrying, i.e., making union with God. The serpent said to her, in effect, that the road to God was through acquiring the characteristics of God. To be like God and to be God are not the same. Eve and Adam were already like God by the fact they existed. By analogy we are like God by virtue of our existence. Like Adam and Eve, we too must curb the desire to covet, for the consequences of not doing so can lead to desolation of ourselves and our planet.

After Eden: Cain and Abel
Birth of the Will to Power

Cain and Abel are the older and younger sons respectively of Eve, born after the expulsion from Eden. The significance of this story centers on their relationship to God, while no mention is made of their relationship to Adam and Eve. As the story unfolds, we find Cain becoming jealous of Abel, whom God seems to favor. His jealousy turns to homicide. When God asks Cain after the deed where Abel is, Cain gives the now famous answer, "Am I my brother's keeper?"

Cain was a farmer and a vegetarian. Abel tended sheep and ate meat. When they brought the fruits of their labor as an offering to God, Cain brought fruits of the earth whereas Abel brought sheep. The latter offering found favor in God's eyes and He made it quite clear to both of them that Abel's offering was favored. Cain became full of wrath and took it out on Abel by slaying him. Abel was an innocent being. He, as the younger brother, did not intend to be competitive. He offered what he had to offer, as custom demanded.

Abel offers the *first fruits* of the flock. That is, he gave to God the best of what he had, whereas Cain does not offer the first fruits. Here Cain betrays the sign of greed, hoarding the first fruits for himself instead of generously offering them up. To offer first fruits is a sign of humility, a practice of humility, and a practice of the vow of poverty. Any giving away, renunciation, divesting, absenting oneself from material gain, clearing a space, throwing out what has been collected, sharing one's largesse, detaching from all attachments to things or to thoughts, are but some examples of practicing poverty. Abel shows he is able to do that while Cain can't.

At first, God rebukes Cain and tells him that while he has acted reproachfully, he still has the will to change direction and straighten himself out. Cain responds by murdering Abel after becoming depressed and angry, two characteristics of the false self. The false self expresses itself on the emotional level by our experiencing distressing mood states and feelings. Both states are examples of blame, either self (depressed) or others (anger). There is practically no distressing experience in the world that is not an example of false-self activity. Investigation of these experiences will always reveal some story about the illusory future, the dead and buried past, or some aspect of the defiant or compliant self, save the acute grief felt when a loved one dies and the subsequent deep mourning that follows (usually from one to three months).

After Cain's act is discovered, he is exiled from his homeland and must wander throughout the world. He was marked on his forehead by God, not only to indicate to others he was a murderer, but also to warn others not to harm him, as dire consequences would befall anyone who would do so. As time proceeded, Cain became the richest man of his time and built an entire city for his son. At the time of the great flood, the entire line of Cain's family was destroyed.

Cain and Abel represent the seed story for all wars, revolutions, and revolts in the world. It becomes clear throughout the story that Abel is favored by God and he can be regarded as a person of higher evolutionary development from a spiritual point of view. His name even means "close to God." Abel is more in tune with what we might call the "true self" nature of our human beingness, while Cain is connected with what we may call the "false self" characteristic of our nature. Just as there are external fratricidal wars raging everywhere in the world ceaselessly — brother murdering brother — so there is the ceaseless inner war going on between the false self(ves) and the true self.

The aim of all wars is based on domination and subjugation of one group by another. The roots of this urge are envy and the urge to be important at the expense of others so as to avoid inferiority. The commandment in question here is the Tenth — don't covet. The vow in question not being addressed is poverty. Coveting has greed at its base, and greed is the result of not following the vow of poverty. Envy, as a form of coveting, fits in directly here because it has always to do with wanting what someone else owns, whatever that object might be.

Cain and Abel's story is the primordial one, the prototype for every relationship in the world regarding the consequences of envy, greed, and jealousy. Jealousy is a three-party relationship, in contrast to envy, which is two-party in nature. Jealousy revolves around relationships where the jealous party wants to possess one of the two others in the triad who may be, or who are in fact bonded to each other. Cain was definitely jealous of Abel's relationship with God.

What is the root of jealousy? I believe it has to do with a commonly shared mass conscious false belief that it is important to be important. We are constantly prompted to "be somebody," to strive, to make a name for ourselves. Conversely, we are told that to be "a nobody" is to be a "loser," an outcast. Being somebody is intimately associated with acquiring status. Status is registered by two criteria: acquisition of money and/or fame. Acquiring money brings the greed factor into prominence immediately. Greed means wanting more, wanting better, wanting different. Being able to wield power through money gives someone a special status in the manmade world.

As becoming important is significant on an individual basis, so has it significance in the larger community.

Countries have wanted to demonstrate their superiority, their importance, by showing how strong and mighty they are, as we have witnessed so painfully in this century through the aggression and atrocities committed by Germany and Japan in the name of claiming aspirations to world dominance. What is fascinating here in the stories of Germany and Japan is that in keeping with the story of Cain's fratricide, they have become two of the richest, if not the two richest nations on earth as a "reward" for their violence, cruelty, and murder.

And so it was with Cain. After the murder and being marked by God, he was sent away from the possibility for spiritual self-mastery and no longer permitted within the precincts of God. What became of Cain was that he subsequently became the builder of cities and with that became the richest man in the world. What a twist to this morality tale. How do we account for the fact that those who commit murder become "rewarded "in this way? Is it in fact a "reward" from the spiritual point of view, or is it in fact a punishment?

From the point of view of spiritual development, the acquisition of material goods is regarded as an impediment. It is inevitable that in fulfilling this impulse, we become identified with the objects we possess. We begin to see no difference between "who I am" and "what I have." Thus, we are forced to expend enormous energy holding onto what we have for dear life because to lose what we have becomes tantamount to losing ourselves. Such expenditure contributes mightily to our decay and demise.

Ultimately, when what we supposedly own flees from us, we feel absolutely bereft, become depressed, and eventually give up interest in life. The mistake of equating what we have with who we are invariably brings pain and suffering, often to the point of intolerability and inconsolability. Additionally, by becoming wedded to material life, it usually happens at the sacrifice of an attunement to the world of invisibility, which is the repository of all the enduring happiness we could know. It has been a commonly known experience that acquisition of material goods has often brought with it a sense of pleasure, well-being, and happiness that is generally short-lived. This is followed by a mounting sense of nervousness and worry about preserving it and/or expanding it. It doesn't take too long before the greed factor sets in, pushing us to want more, better, and different.

For many, the acquisition of money drives them mad. They often end up as drug or alcohol addicts, mentally deranged, or megalomaniacs. Addictive substances themselves pose another danger by becoming an object of adoration or worship. Money becomes a substitute for God, and becomes an object of idolatry; money becomes God.

Of course, the nature of all material life thus far is transience. Materiality is marked by the characteristic of impermanence. It comes and goes. It always passes. We have to recognize the ever-changing nature of the world in which we live and in the midst of appreciating that all is change, come to an awareness of that which never changes, the permanence behind the impermanence. This permanence we call God. God is a never-ending fount of pleasure and happiness which cannot be purchased for any sum of money. However, when I cannot turn toward that reality, and instead dedicate the bulk of my energies to acquiring what's geared to making me important and of status, then I have forgotten God, and have sacrificed my possibility for happiness and freedom, the very things we are all seeking. *The error is to believe that freedom and happiness are centered in material life.* The punishment is that the more we are mired in material life, the more impossible it is to extricate ourselves from it, and the more remote we become from God.

Since the industrial age began, roughly five hundred years ago, a new belief system asserted itself in concert with the rise of industrial life and the development of the capitalist economic system accompanying it. This belief was that life would become easier, more convenient, and that we would be able to live an easily accessible comfortable life. Each new invention, each new discovery about the world around us was to add to the ease and satisfaction that life was to afford us. Convenience, ease, comfort, pleasure were to make life simpler, and ultimately to give us freedom from the toil, hardships, and deprivations suffered by our ancestors. We were to become a world of Faustian men and women where eventually every whim could be satisfied at an instant of wishing it.

This political-economical fairy tale has proved to be just that — a fairy tale. Life is becoming more expensive and complex to keep up with than ever before, and the debilitation brought about by long-term chronic disease makes life not worth living for many millions of people. All of this suffering can be laid at the doorstep of the perpetuation of the false belief that the purpose of living is to get pleasure and to avoid pain. As long as this belief is adhered to, it is virtually impossible for the troubles besetting this earth to cease. By not facing the pain confronting us, we can never resolve our difficulties in living on earth.

As I indicated above, Cain becomes a builder of cities. Cain actually redeems himself by becoming a builder, a constructor. He makes the move from farming to city building much the same as European and American life evolved from the inception of the industrial revolution. At the same time the hunter-gatherer societies have essentially disappeared from life on earth. This shift to an urbanized, technologically based society has been associated with the urge to dominate and subjugate nature to feed the "hungry ghosts" of industrial life. Thus we have lost a wealth of knowledge about the rhythm and cycles of nature from which we could learn a great deal about cycles and rhythms of our own bodies. There are enormous implications here for our health maintenance and regulation.

With the domination of nature has come a breakdown in/of nature so serious that perpetuation of life on earth is imperiled.

Cain thus embodies the movement of entropy, stasis, and breakdown on the planet, which has become the dominant mode of life as we enter the twenty-first century. We are now entering a new turning point where a new order may emerge, bringing with it the building up of life and genesis of the new creative spark that will replace the destructive impulse now dominating the landscape of life in the world.

God in His infinite love allows Cain to make the corrections to redeem himself in spite of himself because everyone deserves a chance at correcting errors, no matter how grievous. God is always giving a chance for evil to turn to good.

The word "correction" is highly important to Western spiritual practice. It means that something that has been incorrectly done can be set straight and we may make compensation to bring us from impurity to purity. We are constantly making errors in this world. That is why I am opposed to the nomenclature of psychology and psychiatry where they set themselves up as the arbiters of everyone's errors, implying that they are free of committing such errors. It is only others who are "dysfunctional," meaning errors in functioning. The truth is that the world and almost the entirety of the world's population is "dysfunctional," including those who would arrogantly judge others' behavior. Errors are of three sorts: those made in ignorance, the sins spoken of in biblical writing; those made knowingly, the transgressions of biblical writing; those made knowingly, maliciously and with the intent to injure, the iniquities of biblical writing. All can be corrected on an individual and communal basis. Correction becomes a necessity then in the mission that a "chosen people" (meaning anyone who chooses to be part of the chosen) has in sharing their wisdom of making corrections to help bring about healing in the world, and by doing so making this world the divine Eden it is meant to become.

I think it is helpful here to bring in two other words of equal import to "correction." They are: "repentance" and "reversing." Repentance has a number of meanings spiritually that don't necessarily accord with the strict dictionary definition. The Hebrew term is "tshuva" (teshoova, phonetically), coming from the root, "to return." Thus, we are turning towards God, away from the path of death. We are taking an action to change our course in life where Spirit has been forgotten or diminished. The English definition of "repent" is to think again, or rethink what you have been doing. The return to God is intimately associated with a major correction involving all Three Vows and the Ten Commandments simply by choosing to make the turn.

There can be no return when we are severed from the sacred. Certainly, the modern world is unrepentant. There is little contrition shown by either cold-blooded killers who dot the American scene, the large corporations who have polluted the natural landscape, and bring high mortality and chronic illness in their wake, the terrorists, organized and otherwise, who have little regard for the holiness of human life. But the door is always open to take definitive action, which inheres in the word correction.

The third term, "reversing," is what repentance and correction are all about. Reversing is a guiding principle for the spiritual activity associated with taking the Three Vows. To become obedient means reversing individuality and placing yourself at the service of the group and its collective good. It is the triumph of altruism over narcissism. To become impoverished or simple requires reversing the acquisitive and hunting habits with which we have been imbued from infancy onward. It is the triumph of giving over getting, of true philanthropy over hoarding. To become chaste finds us needing to reverse our attachment to sexual pleasure for its own sake and take that energy to teach and guide others instead of exploiting them. It is the triumph of friendship and love over self-indulgence and deceit.

* * *

Fratricide can be stemmed by brothers' understanding and assuming their correct roles in the family. The older brother commands respect by dint of his position. The older, by the same token, has to be able to accept what the younger, who can often be wiser, may have to impart. The younger has to be able to impart knowledge without threatening the older that his position and status will be usurped. In this way the impulses of jealousy and envy are brought under control. Since these impulses eventually lead to murder and war, the latter will also be brought under control.

ABRAHAM: THE MAN OF FAITHFUL RIGHTEOUSNESS

Abraham is the father of what eventually became the Jewish people. He is also considered the great father of the Arabs as well. He lived approximately four thousand plus years ago, and had the first recorded awareness and revelation of One God. This event has served as the basis of the creation of Western monotheism. What he discovered was the existence of a One, an invisible reality, having no form, of limitless nature, to which the name God has been appended.

Abraham exemplifies faith and serves as our model for this quality. Faith means, in one context, the certainty of the reality of God. His great revelation had to do with the recognition of one God, i.e., Monotheism. He realized that the worship of deities was an act of enslavement and that in transcending these deities he offered an opportunity to achieve freedom; for to worship God required no indenturing of ourselves, no impoverishment of our personal resources to placate the deity, and eventually no sacrifice of human life to appease the deity. He was the great exponent of negating idol worship and all the subjugation that brings. In fact, one of the momentous acts of his life was to smash the idols of his father, Terah (pronounced Terach), who was a craftsman of figurines in the land of Haran, where Abraham was born. He followed the Second Commandment here of not worshipping nor erecting idols and of not making graven images.

Following directly upon breaking the idols, and in line with enacting his immense revelation of Monotheism, he set out on a journey to take his family, including his wife Sarah, plus his servants, cattle, and goods, to go to the land of Chaldea, a place that was in no way equal to the luxury and magnificence of Ur, the great city of Haran. After reaching Chaldea, he then returned to Ur by the same route he followed from Ur.

There are three important elements about his undertaking this journey. In leaving Ur he was giving up the luxurious, material life for a more simple way of life. He took a vow of poverty emblematically by this act of migration, and as we find out later on, he also enacts obedience and chastity, not to mention humility.

Secondly, he followed faithfully his revelation without wavering. As we see later on, he does the same thing when God asks him to sacrifice Isaac. He listened to his inner voice of intuition by leaving Ur as he later gave ear to God's voice who commanded him to sacrifice his son.

Thirdly, he went and returned by the same route, i.e., he migrated. The great enlightened Hellenistic Jewish philosopher Philo recognized the reference to this migration as an inner one, alluding to a spiritual journey. When the inner path to freedom is taken, we loosen our attachment to the idols of this world. When this migration is happening, we are losing our anchor to the habitual life. After we have made the inner turn, we cannot stay there but have to come back to the everyday reality. In the West, everyday reality is of singular importance, even though it is a place where very little of importance is happening. Most of everyday life is a manufactured reality governed by the will to power and operating by manufactured pseudo-events that rarely, if ever, serve the public good. However, it does serve to draw our attention to participate in it rather than retreat from it. We do so to try and effect a healing of what is essentially a diseased and perverse life without being sucked into it.

In order to be able to plunge into life without being corrupted by it, we must first prepare ourselves, by our own inner work, viz., making this inner migration to learn about the realm of love. We bring this love then back to this corrupting place to influence the world of power. The way proposed by Abraham, who was said to have also taught the children of the East, reminds me of the Zen adage: when at first starting the practice of Zen, mountains are mountains, rivers are rivers, trees are trees. Then with the inner turning, mountains are no longer mountains, rivers are no longer rivers, trees are no longer trees. Upon returning from the inner dehabituated state, mountains again are mountains, rivers are rivers, trees are trees . . . *but* they can now be seen in a new way.

Abraham is recommending a similar path except that when returning to the material world, it is not only perception that is changed, but also are actions in/on the world. This theme is echoed later on by Moses, who leads the people out of bondage and the world of the senses exemplified by the land of Egypt, to freedom in a desert, where there's the virtual absence of material temptation. So, it is necessary when returning to this world that we come back to an anchored reality in this everyday life, and in the same physiological and biological state with which we started. We don't want to be in shock, or to be disoriented in the world, which may happen if we don't return by the same route. Doing so assures us that we can return safely to this everyday human existence.

When Abraham gets to be one hundred and Sarah ninety, they are visited by three angels dressed as humans who come as strangers to their tent in the desert. Abraham greets them with open arms and offers them food and shelter, bespeaking his enormous generosity. Abraham embodies love and kindness: loving your neighbor as yourself and receiving everyone in peace and with a quality of generosity. He shows us the way to make peace not war, and the way toward living in harmony with each other. The angels reciprocate his act by blessing them and telling Sarah she would have a child. She laughs upon hearing this, thinking that child-bearing was impossible at her age. Nonetheless, she does bear a child, named Isaac, which means "he who laughs."

Abraham and Sarah are the model of a married couple. They are a righteous duo who respect each other, protect each other, and put each other first. They display all the qualities that make a marriage possible. For it is the institution of marriage that has been so confounding to modern life. Much as it has had to survive the assault of corporate life which has vied with the spouse for the affection and loyalty of its employee. The pull toward adultery has been great. Modern man has had to choose between his spouse or his mistress in the guise of his corporate employer, or try to maintain both. The modern woman is no longer able to depend on the stability of the man to support a family. Finding men less inclined themselves toward having children and family life, they have sought to become more independent and self-sufficient and consequently less inclined toward having children and family life. It is difficult not to succumb to the pulls of the herd mentality that demand conformity to whatever institution has cowed it into submission. The threats to our safety, comfort, and security intimidates us to surrender our better judgment and to give away our freedom.

But, marriage is a necessary relationship because it is a stage upon which we can practice the vow of chastity, to be faithful to one. If we can't be faithful to one here on earth, it is highly unlikely we can be faithful to the One above.

Abraham was originally called Abram and Sarah Sarai. The *H* was added to each of their names as a sign of their attainment as spiritually realized beings. In the esoteric wisdom of Judaism, all creation derives from a single unpronounceable word that is the name of God. This word is comprised of four Hebrew letters, one of which corresponds to the letter *H* in English. In later Christianity, the relationship of the word to creation is emphasized in the Gospel of John, who says, "In the beginning was the Word, and the Word was with God, and the Word was God" (John 1:1).

With the addition of the *H,* Abraham moves to a higher plane of development. It is here that he is put to a new challenge, the sacrifice of Isaac. Before exploring this story it is instructive to note that as we progress along the ladder of self-mastery, we are always given challenges that match the level to which we have reached. Thus, the higher we go, the greater the difficulty.

In preparation for what Abraham is about to face, God tests him by calling to Abraham, and the latter answers, "I am here" or "Here I am" (either is appropriate). This phrase was his expression of faith and openness to God (unlike Cain, who tried to hide from God), displaying a willingness to follow the One voice no matter what. The "no matter what" in this instance was the command to sacrifice Isaac.

When Isaac is thirty-seven, Abraham is told by God to sacrifice Isaac. Abraham accepts God's directive without question. He takes Isaac to a mountaintop, builds an altar, and binds him. As he lifts his knife, God stays his hand, Isaac is spared, and Abraham passes the test as the great man of faith.

* * *

I am frequently puzzled when people recoil at hearing the story of Abraham and Isaac and the proposed sacrifice of the latter at the hands of the former. I am puzzled because parents have been sacrificing their children for millennia to satisfy the blood lusts of maniacal leaders, and help line the pockets of avaricious merchants of war who stand to profit enormously from the sacrifice of human fodder. Child sacrifice in one way or another has been with us forever. Child murder is one of the oldest crimes known to us and goes on relatively unabated throughout the world. Even today, China has a "secret" policy of murdering girl children and second children of Chinese families, not to mention their slaughter of Tibetan children.

One of the great Hebraic contributions to Western civilization was to introduce rituals and ceremonies designed to quell the murderous impulse that is a basic instinct in human life to this time. Ceremonies such as sacrificial offerings of animals and circumcision of boys at eight days old are examples. Human sacrifice was sought to be abolished altogether.

So, the historical, literal piece of Abraham and Isaac's story reverberate today. Ah, but their story takes on one crucial twist: Abraham does not sacrifice Isaac. Indeed, one of the major moral message of the story is the curbing of the impulse to murder and thus follow the dictum of the Sixth Commandment: Don't murder.

There is a significant spiritual message here as well because Abraham — like Job who follows him over a thousand years later — is given a test of faith and obedience. He is asked by God — like Adam and Eve, who preceded him — to give ear only to the One voice and obey a command without question. Like any true student of a Master, he knows what is being asked of him is for his own good and for his spiritual development. Interestingly, Isaac doesn't question what is going on and is ready to submit to his father's wishes. Isaac is also of great faith who trusts his father Abraham, just as Abraham trusts his spiritual father, God.

I want to draw a distinction here between sacrifice and murder. Sacrifice has to do with forfeiting something of great value for something of even greater value. There is a sacred element embedded in sacrifice; indeed, the word *sacrifice* is derived from the word *sacred*. Sacrifice is done for the sake of a higher purpose, higher value, for others. Murder is obviously everything opposite to what is inherent in sacrifice. Everything about murder is for purposes of self-inflation, for some grandiose motive. The Sixth Commandment makes a clear distinction about this when it says don't murder. And, killing is not murder. When Abraham's hand is stayed against Isaac, he spies the ram caught in a thicket whom he sacrifices to God instead of Isaac. A ram is killed, not murdered. The murderous impulse is transformed and the animal offers himself for that purpose. The ram appears suddenly when it wasn't there before, and comes just at the moment when he is needed. Prior to that, there is no ram, nor any animal. Indeed, Isaac asks before he is bound where is the animal for the sacrifice.

I submit that it is a deep mystery why animal sacrifice is necessary at all to help in quenching the impulse to murder. Certainly, this impulse can find other channels of expression. I know of a person who channeled his impulses into becoming a butcher. Another person became a surgeon. In each instance, a knife had to be put through flesh. The American indigenous peoples used regulated hunting as a means of dealing with the murderous impulse. It is told of in Indian lore that the hunter discovers the animal he is to slay as his pursuit is ended when the animal — like the ram mentioned above — offers himself in waiting for the hunter to inflict the sacred execution.

There can be no denying that the impulse to slay exists in the heart and soul of mankind (not womankind really). It is a fact of life and the community needs safeguards and regulations to harness it. I believe that animals have served the purpose of providing the object of that impulse. Since the murderous impulse has been unharnessed, unleashed, and has run absolutely wild in the twentieth century, we have also witnessed the wanton destruction of the animal population of the world in a way never seen before. We have lost the sacred in life, especially in the last three or four centuries, and we are seeing the horrifying consequences of desacralizing the world. Without the sacred in life, there is no way to rein in the murderous impulse. Without the sacred there is no way to curb any of those five dark currents of the human will: the desire to be great, to take, to keep, to advance, and to hold onto at the expense of others. It is out of these five currents that all human suffering is inflicted from one to another. The presence of the sacred permits us to abandon the desire to be great, while sacrifice permits us to give up rather than to take, keep, advance at the expense of others, and hold onto at the expense of others.

Becoming sacred to/in ourselves requires a wounding of our being rather than wounding others. By this I don't mean hurting or harming ourselves, such as happens in self-mutilation or in committing suicide. Personal sacrifice is a form of self-wounding which has to be done in the service of forgoing the urge to fulfill sensory gratification. We already have wounds present in our bodies. These are our sensory organs: the eyes, ears, nose, mouth. They are discontinuities in the skin covering our bodies, disruptions in the surface. Not only are they the wounds, they also are the organs that push us toward sensory gratification. They receive the stimuli from the world. As such, they have to be trained in a way that doesn't prompt us to continuously seek sensory pleasure. In the service of the Three Vows, curbing sensory pleasure satisfies the fulfillment of all of them. We literally don't blind ourselves, or cut out our tongues. However, we curb our appetites through asserting our will to not fulfill what our perceptions espy. Sacrifice means giving up something we hold precious for attaining something more precious. In this way we sacrifice our tendencies toward tyranny, debauchery, greed, to receive the riches and rewards of the life of Spirit, a matchless experience on this earth.

Those characteristics of taking for oneself, holding onto, keeping, and advancing, incidentally, have to do with the left and right hand, left and right leg, as these are the organs associated with these qualities. It is this esoteric knowledge that was taken up by Christianity in depicting their saviour Jesus Christ as the crucified one who suffered the wounds of the hands and feet by the nails of the Romans. It was not by chance that the renderings are shown in this way. The message was being sent that sacrifice entailed the "crucifying" of these tendencies.

Why is sacrifice so important? Because it is a preparation for taking the leap to Spirit, for we can't climb the ladder of self-mastery unless we sacrifice in the service of the Three Vows. What I am suggesting here is a daily practice of sacrifice, downsizing desires for the sake of finding God. Every day forfeit something precious to you in terms of a personal predilection, and have no regrets, recriminations, or second thoughts. Accept the wounding graciously without complaint. The pain is necessary. It's a new birth into freedom. The birth process is necessarily painful. Remember, Eve was told that the birth process would have to be painful as a consequence of the error made in Eden.

LOT'S WIFE: FROM RIGHTEOUSNESS TO REGRET

Our next story is of Lot and his wife. Lot is Abraham's nephew, who is living with his wife and children in the city of Sodom adjacent to the city of Gomorrah. During the course of their lives there, these two cities became corrupted and degenerate. In Western civilization, these cities are synonymous with wickedness, injustice, promiscuity, cruelty, hedonism, and inhumanity. They model how the world works in general: injustice abounds and perversity is consistently rewarded. For example, the three largest businesses in the world are: arms dealing, drug smuggling, the Mafia. In the U.S. the Mafia is the third largest money-making institution, behind drug companies and the auto industry.

Sodom and Gomorrah, as a single situation in history, stands for the entirety of all the injustice that ever was, is, and will be until the will to power is replaced in human endeavor.

All the degeneracy was not lost on God, who spoke to Abraham and told him that these cities would be destroyed unless ten righteous men could be found who would become the foundation upon which a new social order could be constructed. Abraham was unable to find the ten requisite men, and God mandated the cities to be destroyed. He permitted Abraham's nephew, Lot, and his family to leave. Lot was given this privilege because he gave shelter to two angels who passed by his house. In this regard, he emulated his uncle Abraham, who gave food and shelter to the three angels who visited him and Sarah in the desert many years earlier. The angel warned Lot that no one in his entourage was to look behind at the city they just left. Lot's wife, unable to resist, feeling the loss of what she had always known throughout her life, turned to look and was, without further delay, turned into a pillar of salt. Lot's wife's decision served as an important lesson for everyone to be cognizant of if we want to live a long healthy life, physically and mentally.

Lot's wife is the archetypal story of *regret,* and the way we are all bound to live our relationship to the past. To climb the ladder of ourselves, we have to relinquish our attachments to our personal past and the usual pain and suffering that focusing on these memories can bring. The first evokes feelings of loss of what we once had but have no longer; what we never had and are sad about what we missed; recriminations about the errors we've made; decisions we "should have" made but didn't, and on and on it goes. Remaining anchored to the past keeps us in illusion, constantly mired in what is fundamentally dead, buried, over, finished, ended. Resuscitating the personal past, keeping the illusion alive, keeps us away from the present moment — the region of no-time, the place of God.

The story of Lot's exodus from Sodom and Gomorrah was granted him because he was a righteous man who did not indulge in the idolatrous behavior of the people there. God did require that Lot and his family not look back at what they had just left. Spiritual evolution necessitates that we do not engage in idolatrous behavior — seeking for pleasure in the material world, substituting and craving that pleasure, while excluding our search for pleasure in the invisible world, the realm of God — and to not turn from what is here now to what isn't here anymore. Don't turn away from God.

Lot's wife, having free will and choice, as we all have, was pulled toward reminiscences about what she was giving up, what she supposedly was losing. She was also drawn by the desire to "rubberneck," to look at the site/sight of some destruction taking place. She turned to look and cried voluminously at what she saw taking place, and at the remembrance of what she no longer had or could have. She and her family were heading into an uncertain future. She was impelled to want to cling to what was familiar and certain, even though it was a life filled with injustice and inequity all around her. For most of us, the familiar, painful as it may strike us, is usually more acceptable than heading into the unknown darkness of uncertainty. Sad thoughts are usually mixed with feelings of regret. Regret weaves a web of paralysis around us that inhibits us from taking action and leaves us sapped of energy and unwilling to mount sufficient will to overcome the inertia regret can cause. Tears of regret are full of salt, the main ingredient that leads to sclerosis — hardening — in general, and arteriosclerosis in particular.

When there is a build-up of salt, and other minerals, in the vascular arterial system, it loses its flexibility and resiliency. Eventually, these hardened vessels are not able to pump sufficient blood, containing as it does the necessary oxygen our tissue requires to function properly. There are numerous ill-health consequences for this state of affairs, amongst them heart disease (the leading cause of death in the United States), and Alzheimer's disease, a ubiquitous ailment affecting the brain and disrupting our mental functioning. Such hardening leaves us facing a future that is quite limiting, static, and ultimately life-threatening. Here we can also recognize that sclerosis, hardening on the physical level, is an analogy to regret on the emotional level.

The story of Lot's wife informs us as to what awaits us if we insist on holding onto the past instead of greeting what confronts us now. The mood state accompanying holding on to the past is called "depression." Depression is considered to be self-murder, a partial and progressive suicide thought to be by my teacher, Colette, the gravest error that an individual can commit.

It is self-murder that Lot's wife engages in by looking back. The consequences of this behavior is graphically depicted by what happens to her — an irreversible effect.

Do not think that sclerosing was a punishment visited on her by God. That is not the way it works. It is necessary to dispel this myth perpetuated by some organized religious groups. When we turn away from God — whose existence is experienced right here in the moment, in the realm of the instant, or as modern physics has termed it, "no time," — we forget HIM. When we forget, we in turn are forgotten by God. We are not remembered. We become lost in the world and become prey to the destructive influences of the serpent

that are rife in the world. By shedding our protective shield —
remember what King David writes in the Twenty-third Psalm:
"Yea, though I walk through the valley of the shadow of
death, I will fear no evil, For Thou art with me; Thy rod and
Thy staff, they comfort me" (Psa. 23:4) — we fall prey to the
predators. In effect, we bring the consequences and punish-
ments on ourselves.

We humans are not meant to die. We were not intended
by God to perish and to live in pain, suffering, misery, and
torture. Recall that Adam and Even lived in an eternal paradise, which we are meant to restore here on earth. We, however, have been imbued with the incredible gift of free will
and choice, enabling us to decide for ourselves our own destiny. The great paradox here is that while God authors and
directs the grand cosmic plan, of which we are a part, we
have the authority to determine our role in that plan. We can
choose to live and join God in the grand design, or we can
choose to die and remove ourselves from the grand plan: In
Deuteronomy 30:15-18: "See, I have set before thee this day
life and death, good and evil, in that I command thee this day
to love the LORD thy God, to walk in His ways, and to keep
His commandments and His statutes and His ordinances;
then thou shalt live and multiply, and the LORD they God
shall bless thee in the land whither thou goest to possess it.
But if thine heart turn away, so that thou wilt not hear, but
shalt be drawn away, and worship other gods, and serve
them; I denounce unto you this day, that ye shall surely
perish, and that ye shall not prolong your days upon the
land . . ."

If we choose *against* Lot's wife and don't look back, we
may give ourselves the opportunity to *never* turn into a pillar
of salt, never sclerose, age, or die. Interestingly, sociological
research has revealed that people who live over 100 years of
age share an element in common — the ability to bear loss
well. That is exactly what Lot's wife was not able to do. She

cried for and over the past, was attached to the things of this life, did not realize the inherent transitoriness of the physical objects of this world that we humans desperately seek to acquire and hold onto, and subsequently cried herself to death.

JACOB: THE STORY OF SELF-TRANSFORMATION

As noted in the story of Abraham and the sacrifice of Isaac, the monotheistic civilization strove to eliminate the sacrifice of the firstborn and of the murderous impulse. Along with this abolition the Bible introduced the laws of inheritance designed to create an orderly transition of family hierarchy from generation to generation. Under these laws the eldest members of the family were entrusted with not only the family material goods but also the transmission of the family's spiritual teaching. The eldest son was the guardian of the spiritual teachings.

Alternatively, in the mythology of the West there is a recurrent theme of the sacrifice of the firstborn and of the younger sibling surpassing the older in personal development. We see this theme operating in Jacob and Esau as in Cain and Abel. The former were twins, born to Rebecca and Isaac, Jacob coming out after Esau holding Esau's heel. There seemed to be a struggle in utero as to who would be born first, as Jacob's action would attest.

The twins represent the two sides of our personality: Esau, the one wanting to serve Mammon, the god of acquisitive material life, the other, Jacob, wanting to serve God. Both impulses are at play in all of us. Regarding the latter, there is in all of us an inborn impulse to worship. In the twentieth century, the Swiss psychiatrist Carl Jung made that observation first, as part of his understanding of human development. And it is true, as true as there being the impulses of sexuality and aggressivity that Freud and his followers asserted were carried with us into this life at birth. The loving reverence that is natural to our makeup is easily manipulated in young children in whatever direction one may wish, especially before the age of seven. In Catholicism it is cited that: give the Church a child before the age of three and they will guarantee the formation of a good Catholic. We are eager to bow down, and this is easily triggered. To be in reverence toward God and to find our way to Spirit, we need to bow to imbue humility in ourselves for something beyond material life.

Actually there was little family trouble in the household of Isaac, Rebecca, Esau, and Jacob until Esau at age forty married two women of Hittite lineage, and so married out of the line of the Hebrews. As it is recorded in the Bible, this act caused a "bitterness of spirit" (Gen. 26:35) to develop in Isaac and Rebecca. By outmarrying, he also literally mixed two different traditions together, one Monotheistic and the other Polytheistic.

Rebecca, like Sarah before her, recognized a set of disturbing characteristics earlier in life on the part of an oncoming inheritor that speaks ill of his character and warns them to take an action to head off the trouble. Sarah became alert to Ishmael, Abraham's firstborn son by Hagar the concubine, whom Sarah discovers mocking her natural son Isaac. This humiliating behavior on Ishmael's part prompts Sarah to have Abraham dismiss him from their camp and to send him along with his mother Hagar into the desert. What is behind Sarah's seemingly harsh edict? She is responding to Ishmael's humiliation of Isaac as an act of murder. For it is understood in the spiritual life of the West that to humiliate someone in public was tantamount to committing physical murder. It is a soul murder.

In a somewhat similar vein, Rebecca takes notice of Esau's characteristics and discerns that he has not reached the level where he would merit receiving the transmission of the secret teaching and spiritual wisdom that Isaac has to impart.[3] Esau was a "cunning hunter" and a "man of the field" (Gen 25:27) viz. the material world, while Jacob was quiet and was a meditator, viz., "dwelled in tents" (Gen 25: 27). She then colludes with Jacob to have him impersonate Esau when Isaac is old, blind, and dying, to receive the transmission of the spiritual knowledge.

* * *

In his meeting with angels, he finds them ascending and descending a ladder which is recounted as a dream he experiences. Here we are alerted to the presence of a direction directly associated with spiritual freedom called the *vertical axis,* the movement of up and down.

The vertical axis defines what we call the present moment and limitless space. Freedom can only exist in the now, the presence of the present. This means that we give up our attachment to the past and future. Simply put, whatever goes through our minds that isn't about now keeps us enslaved. It is on the vertical axis that Jacob meets God. God promises Jacob endless seed, and promises to be with Jacob forever and to bring him back to the land of God no matter wherever Jacob may roam. This statement is echoed in the New Testament by Jesus who, in paraphrasing God's comment, says that "I am with you forever, and am never not with you." God promises Jacob and all his descendants to live in the land of God, in the house of God. For Jacob calls the place where he lives the nocturnal vision Beth El = House of God.

On the physical plane, Jacob's ladder represents the movement of the spinal column, the physical ladder of life. In spiritual practice, ascension of the ladder of self-mastery has physical correspondences in sensations experienced at different levels of the spinal column up into the brain and beyond. Additionally, there is another ladder of spiritual centers corresponding to levels of the human body. In the East this is called the Chakra system, corresponding to seven levels of the body beginning in the genital region and ascending to the crown of the skull. In the West this Chakra system is replaced by the system of hormonal organs, thus giving it concrete representation in a locatable anatomical system.

Jacob's encounters with angels represents a story of vast profundity.

It is understood throughout all traditions in the world transculturally that the vertical direction represents the axis of freedom, the ascent that frees us from the constraints, restrictions, enslavement, and captivities that are a necessary part of the world made by/through the hand of man. I say necessary because the world fashioned by us, superimposed as it is on God's handiwork, addresses itself to fostering the will to power expressed as the urge to dominate, subjugate, and enslave so as to elevate oneself to the status of God. Accepting to live by man's rules rather than by God's immediately imprisons our corporeal self and dooms us to a life of suffering, pain, and despair. However, we have been born with the capacity to lift ourselves out of the morass. This happens by refusing to accept the man-made game and turning our interest and attention to God on high.

* * *

The tension between the twins maintains itself throughout their growing up together. Isaac seems to favor Esau, Rebecca Jacob. She had been told by God that he would become the great leader of the people. There are two famous stories associated with them that set the stage for Jacob's later evolution of his character to become the highly evolved and self-realized being he grew into. The first occurred when

Esau came in from hunting in the fields. He was quite hungry and Jacob offered him a bowl of porridge in return for Esau's birthright — his material inheritance. The ravenous Esau, so overcome by hunger, accepted.

The second happened when the dying Isaac, blind and feeble, had to pass on the spiritual transmission intended for his elder son, Esau. Isaac was hungry for meat and Esau went to the fields to hunt game to bring back to his father. At that point Rebecca and Jacob conspired to deceive Isaac. Jacob posed as Esau and fooled Isaac into believing he was Esau. Isaac, believing the ruse, passed the transmission and blessing on to Jacob. When Esau returned, the plot was uncovered but it was too late. Esau was enraged, and Jacob, fearing for his life, fled. It was here that he began his transformation of character.

As he fled to take refuge at his uncle Laban's house, Jacob has his major turning point revelation conveyed through the familiar story of Jacob's ladder. Jacob puts his head on a stone to go to sleep and has a dream where he encounters a band of angels ascending and descending a ladder stretching into heaven.

> Taking one of the stones of the place, he put it under his head and lay down in that place to sleep. And he dreamed *that there was a ladder set up on the earth, and the top of it reached to heaven; and behold, the angels of God ascending and descending on it* (my emphasis).
>
> And, behold, the LORD stood above it, and said, I am the LORD God of Abraham they father, and the God of Isaac: the land whereon thou liest, to thee will I give it, and to thy seed;
>
> And thy seed shall be as the dust of the earth, and thou shalt spread abroad to the west, and to the east, and to the north, and to the south: and in thee and in thy seed shall all the families of the earth be blessed.

And, behold, I am with thee, and will keep thee in all place whither thou goest, and will bring thee again into this land; for I will not leave thee, until I have done that which I have spoken to thee of.

And Jacob awaked out of his sleep, and he said, Surely the LORD is in this place; and I knew it not.

And he was afraid, and said, How full of awe is this place! this is none other but the house of God, and this is the gate of heaven (Gen. 28:10-17).

We find examples of the connection of verticality to the sacred in many traditions: the totem pole in the Shamanic; the tepee in the Native American; the pyramid of Egypt and Mesoamerica; the ziggurat in the Middle and Near East; church steeples in Western religion, to cite a few. In the great sacred symbols of Western spirituality, the vertical is predominantly represented: in the Star of David and the Christian Cross. Also, the essential motto of Hermeticism (the ancient tradition of ancient Egypt and the Mediterranean), embodied in the Star of David, is that which is above is like to that which is below, and that which is below is like that to which is above, to accomplish the miracles of the one thing.

* * *

Once Jacob is attuned, he becomes aware of the existence of angels, the beings who live in this real world or dimension of verticality.

The fundamental answer to life's travail lays in verticality. It is the dimension and realm of God. It is the exit out of the trap of material life and its devotion to finiteness. When my teacher Colette, in our very first meeting, said to me, "In what direction does a train go," after I told her that Freud gave directions for his "fundamental rule" of free association as the key to psychoanalytic treatment by recommending the analyst begin the analysis by telling the patient to imagine being together on a train and repeating everything he sees passing by while looking out the window, I responded by gesturing in the horizontal with my arm and saying, "This way." She retorted by making a vertical upward gesture with her arm and querying, "And if we change the direction?" At that moment I had an awakening to Spirit that forever changed my life. In that pregnant instant she conveyed to me what was akin to Jacob being revealed the vertical cosmology that eventually takes us to God and, ergo, to eternal life.

The experience of angels and of dreams is essential to understanding the wisdom of the ancient world and the timelessness of this wisdom for us. The ancients certainly recognized the reality of angelic existence. They knew quite well that an invisible reality existed because their consciousness believed in the certainty of God. Certainly, most of the ancient world was not Monotheistic. Nevertheless, in their Polytheistic worldview of the time, the reality of incorporeality or invisibility was a given.

This worldview prevailed until about roughly four hundred years ago when the invisible world was removed from the consciousness of Western life. However, they are a fundamental reality of esoteric Western wisdom, and are presumed as such in all the three religious traditions of the West.

The angelic creatures of the air are part of the great chain of being that descends from God. They are of different degrees of density and materiality. Paradoxically, God, of no density, is the *most* concrete reality. Human beings are the most dense but the least concrete of all beings. We are merely an abstraction of/from God, a reflection in vast multiplicity of the all-encompassing unity that is God. Humankind is part of the great chain of Being that begins with God. This chain is comprised of Seraphim, Cherubim, Thrones, Dominions, Virtues, Powers, Principalities, Archangels, Angels, us. We are at the lowest end of the chain and are the most abstract at the same time. The more abstract the less real; the less abstract the more real. All of the beings are real, but the farther we are from God the more tenuous is our hold on reality. When I came to understand this fact I must say that it was truly one of the most humbling experiences of my life.

Yes, we are made in the reflection of God. We are the mirror of the mirror of God through which His Divine countenance is revealed. But, the intermediary beings between us and God all serve specific purposes within the divine hierarchy. For example, the Cherubim guard the tree of life with flaming swords. The closest beings to us are the angels, who are our guardians. Each of us is born with at least one guardian angel. In addition to guarding, angels also cherish, protect, visit, and defend us. In guarding us, the angel guards the memory of our connection between the great yesterday, today, and tomorrow of our soul with respect to its mission to reunite with God. The angel cherishes the quest of the soul engaged on this way. The angel will visit, when it is called for, to take a more active, direct part in human activity, as did the three angels who visited Abraham and Sarah in the desert. The angel can protect us from dangers of all sorts when called upon — an absolute necessity to be done by us — through our prayers and supplications.[4]

In all of the above functions the angels' efforts are directed downward toward activity in the human world. The fifth function of defending also concerns human activity, but it is directed upward into the heavenly court. The esoteric wisdom describes how ceaselessly we are on trial, indictments being brought against us by the prosecuting angels who have marshalled a case against us for our sins, transgressions, and iniquities, and are demanding justice. All that we think, feel, and do is registered in a heavenly record that is opened as "exhibit A" in the heavenly court. We are the essential constructors of our reward or ruin here on earth, and our defense attornies, as it were, make a case for our gaining reward for continued life.

Now, Jacob had direct contact with the angels who are bearing the richness of God to earth, and are carrying up the holy sparks back to God that we too extract from our lives when we live a righteous and pure way. The angels are God's messengers, the "Elohim" spoken of in Genesis, who are designated to be conduits between ourselves and God.

In climbing the ladder of self-mastery, we may be escorted by the angels who would never stand in the way of our pilgrimage to God. They are our escorts to the heavenly altar analogous to our earthly parents who lead us down the aisle to the altar only to step out of the way so the marriage may take place.

We are on this earth for one sole purpose — to serve God, and through our service to marry and become One with God. All of life experience gives us the opportunity for this service that has to be done in His name, not in our name. That is the challenge of earthly life — to replace our name with His name. We are to take the stairway to heaven to establish this union and renounce our claim on proprietorship here.

Jacob becomes aware of the new reality of these angels via the dream, itself a world of reality.[5] Here then are three of the most significant elements of the world of freedom interwoven neatly in a short description of Jacob's experience: the vertical axis, angels, the dream.

After this revelatory dream, Jacob knew his mission in this world was to create a line of people that would fill the world and through them "all the families of the earth [will] be blessed."

Jacob was the man of practice and discipline. This is what is meant by his "dwelling in tents." He set his tents up in the desert into which he consistently entered to do his spiritual practice. He was the model of the disciple whose yearning was squarely centered on God, while at the same time being fully immersed in everyday life. He was a great patriarch who sired twelve children from whom the perpetuation of Monotheism stems, and who carry the remembrance of verticality in their bodies, souls, and spirits. The Monotheistic way is to regard the everyday world with reverence and significance because the practice of its spirituality depends on using everyday life as a reminder to engage the practice of vertical ladder climbing, of which Jacob was a master. By addressing the world in this way and not dismissing its importance, we also feel impelled to serve God and preserve His creation, to act on/in this world to help heal it. The simultaneous twofold action of vertical ascent and horizontal repair on/in the world is unique to Monotheism and gives it its quintessential importance.

Jacob was one of the most blessed beings in world history. He was blessed by Isaac, Laban his father-in-law, the Lord God, and also by the angel he wrestled with at night until dawn. In this latter instance he encounters an angel the night before he is to meet Esau whom he hadn't seen in over 22 years. He wrestles throughout the night with him till the dawn. He did not allow himself to be subdued. Instead he subdued the angel by grabbing hold of his testicles and forced him to give him — Jacob — a blessing. The angel then gave him the name Israel, meaning "struggling with God." To receive a blessing means a spiritual infusion, transmission, or initiation. Following this, Jacob exclaimed, "I have seen God face to face and my life is preserved" (Gen. 32:30). He engaged in the struggle with both humans, viz., Esau and Laban, and with God and prevailed.

Jacob is everyman who bears in his heart the yearning for salvation, redemption, the meeting with God. Such meetings require we radically depart from our ordinary way of life and embrace the out of the ordinary vertical existence, the reality of angels, the significance and importance of dreams, the acceptance of God.

Jacob's struggle is also that of everyman. He goes through a transformation of his being throughout his life until reaching God. He has to face trials and tribulations as that is part of, and is a necessity for the transformative process. Even after receiving the name of Israel that denotes his enlightened status, he still has to endure personal suffering when, much later in his life, he is led to believe that his favorite son Joseph has been killed by wild animals. He has to be able to bear this loss without losing his will to live and giving up on life. The ability to bear loss without losing the will to live for us all is a critical factor for staying in life, since loss in some manner is inescapable and must be faced by everyone. How we handle it is directly connected to longevity.

His struggle with the angel is stated in the Bible to have taken place "at night until the rising of the sun." We have to fight the darkness that both surrounds us and is in us, which we have to root out and purify ourselves in the light of the sun of daytime. The dark is the unknown, the essence of all fear. He had to do it alone. He had sent his family, servants, and goods over the stream Jabbok and remained by himself to undertake the struggle. The struggle with/for spirit is done when the family is safely tended to. The family is not to be sacrificed for personal spiritual growth. They are a responsibility that has to be accounted for and made part of the ladder climb.

It is interesting to note that Jacob's encounter with the wrestler takes place between resolving to meet Esau, and the actual meeting with Esau. Before the wrestling he was afraid of Esau's wrath for having been deceived out of his birthright. When he finally met Esau, he had been dubbed Israel. He was now unafraid. The meeting went smoothly, all of Jacob's fears allayed as they kissed each other, wept, and Jacob graciously gave Esau back a goodly portion of his birthright, noting that God had given him a sufficient portion and now, in turn, such beneficence could easily and generously be given to another. For once having tasted of God's goodness, Jacob had little need for overweening attachment to material goods.

The lesson of Jacob's philanthropy to Esau says a great deal about how we have to treat our brother earthlings, and how it will come to pass when we taste of God's goodness. Until that time comes, selfishness and war remain a way of life in the world. Jacob is not greedy and the absence of this quality speaks to a real inner transformation. With this transformation comes a richness from above that money cannot buy, in fact, money cannot permit us to buy.

For our modern day, one account of the the Jacob-Esau drama is played out in the Near East as Israel gives back land to the Arabs, Esau being one of the sires, along with Ishmael, of the modern Arab world. It just doesn't happen that land won in war or taken by violence, as America did to the indigenous peoples, is given back peaceably. But, we are now witnessing Jacob's (Israel's) reconciliation with Esau. It is up to Esau to accept the offering and to respond with friendship and peacefulness. If Esau does so, which bodes well for the Arab response, that would be a breakthrough for a part of the world that has never been able to live in peace, and has been unable to shed its enmity toward strangers and its ingrained anti-Semitism against its own people of like descent there, and everywhere in the world.

The miracle of relinquishing wrath is the great task of the Arab world. As the prophet Amos said: "Thus saith the Lord: For those transgressions of Esau, Yea, for form, I will not reverse it: Because he did pursue his brother with the sword, And did cast off all pity, And his anger did I fear perpetually, And he kept his wrath forever" (Amos 1:11).

Jacob's transformation awaits everyone who decides to climb Jacob's ladder.

JOSEPH: THE GATHERER, THE ART OF STATESMANSHIP

The story of Joseph and his brothers highlights the story of family life and the relationship of brothers to one another.

Joseph was the eleventh of Jacob's twelve children. He was an especially gifted boy who was given to boasting. He was Jacob's favorite, a fact that did not sit well with Joseph's brothers. In addition, Joseph had a great talent for dream reading. When he was a young man he made the mistake of telling his brothers a dream where their sheaves of wheat were bowing down before his sheaf of wheat standing erect above theirs. The brothers did not take kindly to this either, fearful that Joseph, by dint of their understanding of the dream, would become their lord and master. Naturally, their envy of him was aroused. Envy is the father of anger and grandfather of murder. Joseph's brothers, their ire aroused, conspired to get rid of him. They did so by dumping him into a deep pit where he lay captive until they sold him into slavery to some passing Egyptians. They took Joseph's coat of many colors — an item given to Joseph by Jacob as a sign of the special esteem Jacob had for him — smeared it with the blood of a wild animal, and brought it to Jacob. They told Jacob that Joseph was killed by a lion.

Joseph is indentured to Potiphar. He spurns the advances of Potiphar's wife, who in her wrath has him imprisoned by falsely accusing him of trying to seduce her. While in jail he reads the dreams of two other prisoners, both of whom are servants of the Pharaoh. One of them alerts the king of Joseph's talent, and he is called upon to read a vexing dream of Pharaoh. The dream in sum: seven lean cows devouring seven fat cows; seven lean ears of corn devouring seven full ears of corn. Joseph warns Pharaoh of an impending famine, which prompts the king to take action to store grain for all the people. Pharaoh rewards Joseph by making him the second most powerful man in Egypt. Famine does spread to the land of Canaan, where Joseph's family resides. The brothers go to Egypt and meet Joseph, whom they don't recognize, and beg him for food. Eventually Joseph reveals himself, forgives them, and acts to reunite the entire family, including Jacob, in Egypt.

* * *

As a foolish adolescent Joseph was headstrong and naive. He paid for that. Twenty-two years later he had become wiser as he went through his inner development and matured into a wise counselor and enlightened man. In between he endured slavery and imprisonment in the land of Egypt. In Hebrew, Egypt means "narrow," implying a narrowing of one's existence. This is linked to the esoteric meaning of Egypt as attachment to the senses and to material life. Such attachment represents a narrowing of our life existence. As I mentioned earlier, it is often necessary for the spiritual aspirant to leave the family of origin and their embedded belief systems within the herd mentality to find truth, freedom, and God.

Joseph found his greatness outside of the family, amongst a group of complete strangers who were more receptive to his gifts than his own family.

For us, living now, the circumstances are not much different than they were for Joseph. We are living in the world of Egypt right now. Within this context we have to exile ourselves from the prevailing belief systems promulgated by the false selves. We actively live as exiles from untruth to find our way to truth. Like Joseph, we participate in the life of the community, while using these circumstances as the springboard for conducting our spiritual practice.

* * *

There is more to consider about Joseph's work of dream reading in general, and the theme of the seven fat and seven lean cows. The reading of Pharaoh's dream illustrates a wonderful point about conservation of resources that has meaning on a personal and communal level. At first Pharaoh's dream alludes to the fact that there are seven-year cycles in our individual lives and societal life. In fact, cycles are an integral part of the esoteric wisdom. On a personal level, the ages of our life are divided into seven-year periods: from birth to seven is the age of greatest receptivity where we are our greatest height of absorption of data. We are literally sponges during this time, and it is here that we formulate our worldview so that by the time we come to the beginning of the next cycle — of socialization — from seven to fourteen, we are already accepting only that which conforms to that worldview and are rejecting all that doesn't conform. During the cycle of socialization, we are learning about friendship, alliances, teamwork, and the first real explorations of the world. From fourteen to twenty-one is the time of intellectual attainment and forming of romantic relationships. We are making choices in accord with our philosophy of life and are defining career choices while trying to tame hormonally driven impulses. From twenty-one to twenty-eight, we are establishing our adult direction. This means that we begin to meet the challenge to fight for our own life, and in many cases, our livelihood. At twenty-eight we begin to ripen in our attitudes and are developing our abilities in our life choices such as career, marriage, deeper learning. At thirty-five we enter the phase of maturity. It is here that we sow the seeds that we shall reap in the next seven-year cycle beginning at the age of forty-two. At forty-nine we come to our personal jubilee cycle. Here we may enter a cycle where we reverse our course in life, taking on altogether new possibilities. At fifty-six we begin preparation for spiritual life. At sixty-three we enter into a full-blown spiritual mastery cycle. From age seventy on, we are home-free to enjoy the fruits of our spiritual efforts, and to begin sharing our wisdom and knowledge with those who seek us out.

In defining seven years of feasting followed by seven years of famine on a communal level, Joseph makes a case for husbanding resources, noting that during times of feast we must store resources wisely for the time of famine. Conservation of energy and frugality are qualities we must develop individually and collectively. A balance is needed between spending-saving, production-consuming.

Cultivating frugality, a part of the vow of poverty, teaches us to detach ourselves from attachment to material life. Frugality means not making unnecessary expenditures, thereby maintaining a proportionate attitude toward money. The disproportions concerning money have to be avoided: On the one hand, profligate, wasteful, unnecessary spending, and on the other, miserliness, stinginess, and withholding of funds. The former way makes us unmindful of the possibility of famine and the forces of nature that may come and disrupt our economic lives, sometimes without warning. The latter way makes us ungenerous and unloving, and unable to effect deep, affectionate relationships.

What becomes important in terms of cultivating the quality of frugality is to understand the term "unnecessary" mentioned just above with regard to expenditures. We may want something because the natural tendency of the mind is to desire, to want. This tendency has to have its due in material life because the endless glut of material objects of all variety and stripe that parade before our eyes is mind-boggling. We are stimulated to want at almost every instant. We are the epitome of the unsatisfied, never-to-be-really-satisfied person who has everything at hand but is never satisfied no matter the ease of convenience. The greed factor seems to always wriggle its way into the desiring mind. There is never enough in this materially based life. This desiring mind can be stilled with great effort and concentrated attention, especially if we take our attachment away to the material world.

There is an immense difference between want and need. Yes, it is human to want. But does that want translate into a need? You walk by the shoe store and are taken by a beautiful pair of shoes. You know you have several pairs in your closet. Do you need this pair? Acknowledge your want of/for them and then ask, "Do I need them?" The answer will almost invariably be "no." When it is "yes," the need is certainly valid.

Not only do we have to be aware of how societal standards affect our not being able to soberly determine need, but we are also prodded unendingly by the institution of advertising, where the attempt is to hypnotize us into buying so much of what we don't need. We are hard put to resist the bombardment on our senses, but that is the challenge of frugality. It has to be learned. It is absolutely amazing how the burden of material desire is lifted when frugality is learned. And, it doesn't mean to be cheap, which is closer to miserliness. But, it teaches us to husband our resources, putting us on an even keel so that the fat years can be enjoyed, and the lean years can be enjoyed equally as well. You see, it really doesn't matter whether we are in fat or lean times because our inner resources are available no matter what the external circumstances.

The technological age has produced a wild, unchecked consumerism that has brought about a depletion of resources, extinction of animals, and mass starvation around the world, including our own country. We are a nation in imbalance, devouring everything in sight and using up the resources of the world at a dizzying pace. At the same time we are hoarding other resources, namely, food grains at the expense of the rest of the world, where so many millions are starving to death. These grave imbalances are just now beginning to enter consciousness with a faint glimmer to make us aware of the need to redress them. To redress this immoderation, a balance has to be struck between the promise of individual liberty with the good of the community at large, which may have to override individual desires. Pharaoh does just that. Under Joseph's guidance, the king orders the storage of grain for the good of the community at large, not to line the pockets of a vested few who might benefit from the storage of goods. When the good of the community is borne in mind, we have a practice at hand for counteracting the greed factor, thus allowing us to carry out the Tenth Commandment of not coveting.

※ ※ ※

As for dream reading, the biblical perspective has never been fully elucidated before, although there have been volumes written about dream interpretation. Throughout a good deal of the twentieth century, Freud's *Interpretation of Dreams* served as a model for dream understanding. Freud, however, misunderstood the language of dreams and tried to make the non-rational experience of dream imagery into a rational, verbally based language of everyday waking experience. To try to understand a picture language in logical terms is misguided, and Freud's dream interpretation mode of believing dream images to be a disguise for some underlying wish has been a dismal failure as we come to the close of the twentieth century.

I seek to single out Freud as the "straw man" because he grandiosely fashioned himself to be a modern-day Joseph. He had not the first inkling of what Joseph was talking about; otherwise he would never have juxtaposed himself to Joseph in this way.

Joseph understood the dream as a hieroglyph of the mind, completely in keeping with the world in which he found himself. Egypt was the land of the hieroglyphs, the sacred pictorial language of Pharaonic Egypt. The sacred dream language was a revelatory one, speaking in the true and natural language of the mind called image. It displayed everything in a language that was *analogical,* not logical, one of the very ways that we have set out to read and understand the Bible.

What Joseph's expertise permitted him to do was to be able to read the analogies to which the images of the dream pointed. In fact, when I or my students begin our dream-reading sessions with anyone, one of the first questions we ask is what is the analogy or correlation between the dream experience and what is currently going on his/her everyday life circumstance. By the way, the form of dream understanding in the biblical direction is dream *reading, not* dream interpretation. Joseph read the language of Pharaoh's dream and did not interpret Pharaoh's dream in the way the word is usually understood in modern-day usage, especially in psychology.

Interpretation, as it is commonly used today, means linking the dream experience with some past experience of our personal historical past to which the dream alludes. As well, characters met in the dream are interpreted in terms of important figures in a person's life, like mother or father, no matter who that figure may be — Mahatma Gandhi, Mao Tse-tung, Mae West, or whoever may appear. Interpretation always refers to some preconceived notion of what dream elements describe. Freud's interpretations always referred to a preconceived theory about sexual body parts and other essential

Freudian constructs. In his version, the dream never stood a chance to stand on its own, as it had to be used to support his preconceived theoretical suppositions. The dream had to help save his theory.

Joseph was no such dissimulator. He had no theory to save. He merely looked at what was in front of him and read it as *all* imagery experience is to be read — *analogically* — not psychologically. In the Bible, not one dream — be it of Jacob, Daniel, or whomever — is ever related to some psychological function. Dreams in the Bible always refer to the present condition or circumstance of the dreamer, give solutions to problems or answers to questions, and indicate what's to come.

Thus, the seven cows of Pharaoh in no way refer to a mother figure who existed in Pharaoh's past, as Freud might have postulated. Joseph saw the analogy of the fat cows and lean cows to the state of affairs in Egypt, viz., the welfare of Egypt. Fat cows flourish when the grass is lush and the chewing is good. Lean cows don't do well when there isn't cud to chew, viz., when there is famine in the land. This is clearly what Joseph saw in the moment of Pharaoh's imagery. He read the analogy and communicated that to Pharaoh.

And, as is the case with biblical dream life, the dream is used to provide understanding that will benefit the entire community. For Pharaoh such was the case. Armed with the revelatory knowledge provided by Joseph, he was able to order his bureaucrats to store grain during the good times as a hedge against a time when famine might prevail in the land. In fact, he had them store grain for seven years, according to the number seven appearing in his dream.

The ancients, like Joseph, were well aware of the significance of numbers. The Egyptians were the greatest architects and geometers of the ancient world, and were in possession of the deep meaning of numbers and their place in the grand cosmic scheme of the structure of the universe. Pythagoras, the greatest mathematician of the ancient world, was trained in the Egyptian wisdom tradition (as were Plato and as Moses was before him). In addition, the ancients, being connected to nature and the movements of the celestial bodies, were intimately conversant with the cycles of nature. They tried to live in accordance with these cycles, knowing that the number seven represented a cycle of growth. As well the ancients divided the cycles of human transformation into seven-year cycles.

One particular expression of the seven-year cycle is to be found in the biblical notation of the "jubilee" (Lev. 25:8). The jubilee occurs every 49 years or 7 x 7 = the seventh year of the seventh cycle of seven years. At the time of the Jubilee, a great reversing takes place in the community: all debts are forgiven, the land is not tilled for one year, prisoners are let out of jail. For us as individuals, the age of forty-nine — or the fiftieth year — is a time of great reversing in a person's life. Many people experience a major turnaround in life at this period. I know that I did. At this time, be prepared to change the course of your life.

In looking back on Joseph's life, we can see that he epitomized the gatherer. That is the meaning of his name. His dream was about gathering, and this angered his brothers. In Egypt, where he read the Pharaoh's dream, it had to do with gathering, the gathering of the grains as a hedge against the upcoming famine he foresaw in Pharaoh's dream. Joseph eventually gathered his brothers back together again with him when he revealed himself to them when they came to Egypt begging for wheat. We must all follow his lead to act to cause to come together to bring unity and to join together for a common purpose. He showed how we may use our institutions for the common good.

MOSES: PROPHET, LAWGIVER, THE PATH TO FREEDOM

Moses is the great lawgiver and greatest hero of the Bible. Like many in the heroic tradition, he has to leave home to experience the world away from the habitual environment and to come to the fulfillment of his being. It is then he can return home in a new way and create something significant and special in his community. The history of the world has hinged on individuals whose actions shape and shift the consciousness of mankind. Moses was such a person whose actions created a shift in consciousness of such magnitude, by laying down the foundation for spiritual transformation, rekindling in the soul of the multitude what Abraham had begun but was forgotten in the four-hundred-year enslavement of the Israelites in Egypt. Moses becomes the leader of the Israelites after undergoing eighty years of personal spiritual training begun in Egypt and completed under the tutelage of his father-in-law, Jethro. He shows the slaves the way to freedom, which is detailed in the book of freedom called Exodus. He takes them on a forty-year journey through the Sinai Desert, where they witness many miracles including: the deliverance of the Ten Commandments that convey the law upon which human life is based; and the spiritual realization of 600,000 people at one time at Mount Sinai, a feat that has never been duplicated before or since in recorded history.

The life of Moses is spectacular. He is forced to leave home a few days after his birth because of a decree by the Pharaoh of Egypt, who decreed that every firstborn Hebrew male child be killed for fear that the Hebrews, who were in captivity, would become so numerous that his kingdom would be overrun. Moses's mother saves him by placing him in a reed basket and floating him in the Nile. He is discovered by the daughter of Pharaoh, who, according to the esoteric tradition, picks him up and is cured of a chronic malady. She accepts him as an Egyptian child, takes him as her own, and raises him in the royal court of Egypt, where he is trained in the wisdom of Pharaonic spirituality.

Moses came to recognize the despotism of Egyptian society growing up as he did under the rulership of the Pharaoh, a prototype despot who wanted every firstborn male child slaughtered while slave-driving a whole nation of people to fulfill his megalomanic urges. Megalomania is an irreversible mental disease of *believing* yourself to be God.

Moses didn't sit idly by meekly accepting the aberrant acts of Pharaoh. He understood that there is only one true ruler of this world and that it didn't have human form, and that no power on earth could match it. He woke up! While awakened, he saw that everyone else was asleep, wed as they were to their material desires, to their Egypt. He saw how his brethren, the slaves of Egypt, were being mistreated. At age forty, he kills an Egyptian slavemaster who was savagely beating an Israelite. Living out the law of "mystical ethics," he could not stand by and see the blood of his brother be spilled. He fulfilled a cosmic law when he did that. Interestingly, the slave whom Moses saved was so habituated to abuse that he questioned Moses's action, as though it were natural and to be expected that he be whipped and trampled. But Moses knew better because he woke up. Once he was awake there was no stopping him. He immediately challenged the Pharaoh's authority to enslave others. He brought law and order via the Ten Commandments and the Passover seder meal, the meal of liberation and order (*seder* means order) — to a world in disorder, acting under arbitrary law, satisfying the convenience of those in power at the expense of those not in the "in" group.

After killing the guard, Moses was forced to flee from Egypt. He spends the next forty years amongst the Midianites, coming under the mentorship of his eventual father-in-law, Jethro, the high priest of Midian. Jethro has him become a shepherd. His task is to tend sheep for forty years without losing one. Of course, this shepherding prepared him for the literal historical forty-year-sojourn of the one million people he shepherded and tended to in the Sinai desert, a place where no one of his flock suffered a death except as that brought about directly by God. He took this large group on a spiritual journey, into freedom, into a desert. The habitual could be left behind and sensory attachment is virtually absent. In the desert we truly take the vow of poverty. Yet, this mass of people were fed, sheltered, and clothed for forty years effortlessly.

This is the spiritual side of mastership. To be a guide along the road of spirit, one has to be attentive to his flock to make sure that each person is following his own nature, is safe, and is not going overboard in worshipping or idolizing the master. Such masters exist, and as they are genuine, are not publicly known ordinarily. Of course, if you should want such a teacher, he/she will appear.

It was in the desert that all sorts of "supernatural" events took place: the appearance of the manna, the coming of the quail, the parting of the Red Sea, water issuing from the rock, the cloud that led people through the desert, no one dying of disease, the bestowal of the Ten Commandments, the initiation of 600,000 people at one moment into spiritual awakening.

That so many miracles occurred during this time isn't surprising, as the raised consciousness of Moses, and those intimately associated with him, was able to access the deeper reality that underlies the ordinary perception of our everyday life. In truth, the "miraculous" is the true reality. What we usually perceive is the distortion of that reality clouded over by our own beliefs, opinions, and preconceived ideas that interpret reality according to a fixed logic that supposes that things can only happen in a predetermined way.

The miraculous means that events and experiences happen in a simultaneous, synchronous (happening together =

syn, in time = chrony), acausal (not in the usual time-bound physical experience of cause and effect or past → present → future), not governed by the laws of logic and the laws of historical time. In fact, it is the acausal, non-time-bound, no-time event that has reverberations over time. For example, the miracle of the Red Sea has had an effect in time these past 3,500 years. In the world of the miraculous, anything can happen, since there are no logical constraints. Everything happens spontaneously, and with the creation of our will. This is the true reality, the miraculous truth lying behind ordinary sensory perception. Moses *thought* the Red Sea to part. He was aided perhaps by gravitational pull, perhaps by the first recorded appearance of the planet Venus, shining forth in that night sky 3,500 years ago. Moses prayed; he thought; he willed; *and the universe responded!* That's how miracles work and come into existence.

When my patients image, viz., engage in concretized prayers, prayer given form as image, their prayers can be answered by the universe; by the divine influx; by the universal life force responding to a supplicant's plea. The medical profession often calls these healings "spontaneous remissions," its way of notating miracles. However, I can explain miracles in a way the medical profession can't: a miracle has no antecedent, no precedent, and is not dependent nor contingent on anything known to us already in this world of three-dimensional space and linear time.

* * *

One cogent question that can be raised here is why did the Israelites have to wander for forty years when the distance between Egypt and Israel is so small that the Holy Land could be reached rather quickly from Egypt? The answer to this question actually frames the wisdom to be derived from plunging into the depths of this story.

To leave Egypt is to leave the world of material attachment, the desire to acquire material possessions and make a turn toward Spirit. Moses was a grand spiritual master, who offered a path toward liberation from the enslavement of the senses, which is what spiritual practice is all about. Once we begin to detach from seeking material wealth and chasing after Mammon, we have embarked on a monumental exodus of our own. Making a turn of this sort places us in a new location inwardly that is analogous to the desert of the Israelites. To go to, or to be in a desert is an absolute necessity for spiritual evolution. It is a place that leaves you to be only with yourself, commune, contemplate, and discover truth. They had to become purified and spiritually trained before they could be permitted entry into the holy land.

But why forty years? The number forty has a special meaning (as all numbers do). For Western spirituality, numbers (and geometric shape and colors) are the deepest symbols that we have. The number forty concerning Moses is of especial meaning here. Forty has the meaning of tests and trials. The Israelites spent forty years in the desert; Moses trained for forty years to become a leader of his people. Noah spent forty days in the ark before all the creatures could go back on the earth. Jesus fasted for forty days in the desert. These are some among many examples concerning the number forty, and are sufficient to give the flavor of the profundity of this number. It is not by chance that this number shows up in these events that describe the trials that we humans have to go through to become the master of ourselves, to climb the ladder of ourselves to reach Spirit.

So, the desert wanderers spent forty years cleansing themselves, receiving the way to find eternal life amidst peace, harmony, and love through the gift of the Ten Commandments. They were even permitted to make the necessary correction for the transgression of making the Golden Calf.

The Golden Calf was an idol erected out of the eruption

of the impulse to worship the material over the immaterial. As soon as Moses left the group for a short period to commune with God and receive the Ten Commandments, the group, prodded on by those who joined them in the desert, immediately erected a statue of gold. Idolatry beckons intensely and endlessly. It is a distortion of the *natural* impulse of all humans to worship. It is that impulse that can take us to freedom ultimately. With this impulse we can either choose to worship the limitless invisible reality, or we can choose to worship a limited visible reality, powered by the force of death that demands our life from us in return for the promise of some *future* happiness that is *never* anything but an empty promise.

Changing the direction of the impulse to worship is of significance that our very lives depend on. By changing the direction from visible to invisible reality, we gain the opportunity for ourselves to experience the influx of a cosmic force or light called "grace" to enter us that can forever change our lives. This divine force is called love. That which sends this love is called Truth.

MOSES AND GOLD

When the Hebrews fled Egypt they went with a good deal of gold and jewelry of a precious nature. Why would a group about to take a spiritual journey into the sensory isolation of the desert take those precious material possessions that would seem not to have any value? And, from where did the slaves acquire this gold?

Let's take a deeper look at gold. Gold for the ancients (this also includes the Incas, who were of a similar mindset to the Pharaonic worldview) represented the light of the sun. It was the physical analogy to that light that provides life to this earth As the most precious metal on earth, it has also taken on the meaning of higher transformation of self. In older alchemical terms, it had the meaning of transmutation, the turning of the base metal, lead — the dark metal — having practically no value and being poisonous when ingested, to boot — to the metal of light; gold that is at once medicinal when ingested, is a repository for light, and is altogether health-giving. In our personal transformative work, we want always to turn the lead of illness or base instinctual impulses to the gold of health or creative activity.

As we can see, gold had much more value than the mere material attribution it has now. Even on this level it still stands as the standard against which all the world's money is set. In modern allopathic medicine, gold has been used as a treatment for arthritis and in dentistry as a protection against dental caries.

Gold also has the property of being able to be smelted at high temperature into a white substance or powder that may have been a form of manna that had been thought to allow initiates to enter mystical states and/or to be taken as a curative for disease. Remember no one died in the desert. Could this remarkable event in part be due to the use of this white powder?

Another type of manna was thought to be of the natural variety that came to the Hebrews through the production of a sticky white substance produced by the insect called the aphid, whose secretion could be used for food, which is exactly what the desert wanderers did. This manna might have also cured illnesses.

Additionally, Moses commissioned the goldsmith Bezalel to create a tabernacle of certain proportions to house the Ark of the Covenant. A tabernacle is a portable sanctuary, and the ark is a chest that contains the two tablets Moses brought down from Mount Sinai. Some believed the ark housed the jewelled breastplate of the Great Priest that served the functions of: sending healing laser rays to diseased parts of the body; an instrument of war that could send Buck Rogers, Captain Kirk-like rays at an enemy to kill them; or it could be used in an oracular manner to answer questions posed to it through the flashing of its jewels, much like a modern computer, that the great priest would read for the supplicant. Be that as it may, the sanctuary and the chest were made of gold.

The tabernacle was the forerunner of the *succah,* the booth used to celebrate the harvesting of the fruits of the earth. The celebration is called Succoth (the h is silent), or festival of booths. In ancient days the walls of these booths were constructed of different metallic elements in layers according to a prescribed plan. Gold, silver, copper were used. When one would sit inside such a construction, the ionization created by the intermingling of these elements would produce a great sense of well-being or "high" in the sitter. Sitting in this kind of tent, as Jacob was accustomed to doing in the desert, was a useful way for someone to attain altered states akin to what happens in deep meditation, or in the imaginal experience of the visionary experience of waking dream. In fact, these booths were able to help facilitate this imaginal experience, the way of practice used and taught by the prophets.

Of course, in the desert when Moses ascended Mount Sinai to receive the law, some segment of the people got together and took the gold and jewelry and fashioned the Golden Calf. The ability to create this idol bears testimony to the fact that the means for smelting gold existed in the desert. As soon as the group was left prophetless, the older impulses set in and the reversion to worshipping materialism came bubbling to the surface. This event points up what I have well understood in my thirty-four years of medical practice: impulses are not eradicated nor exterminated. They are controlled and mastered and replaced by constructive habits.

The use of gold for idolatry demonstrates the two-sided nature of almost everything we might employ in life. Every

element has its upside and its downside. What can be beneficially used in one way can be destructively used in another.
For example, cocaine has been used for years medicinally in
medical practice. Employed in this judicious and moderate
way, there is benefit: as a cough suppressant, as a means to
provide anesthesia so that the upper region of the nose and
back of the throat can be examined by various medical
searching devices, as a means to treat intractable pain by a
procedure called sphenopalatine block. On the other side of
the ledger, the destructive effects of cocaine are quite well
known to anyone who has had either direct or indirect contact with large doses of this substance. It is now known that
alcohol in moderation has a salutary effect on heart and vascular system functioning. Used differently, alcohol cuts a
destructive swath through the lives of those associated directly or indirectly with its use. Likewise, gold can help to heal us
or hurt us. The lust for it has been legendary; the Spanish
explorer Pizarro, for instance, whose insane quest for it led to
the destruction of the Inca civilization.

After the Golden Calf, the experience of Moses and the
desert elders led them to fully abandon their prior connection to Egypt by substituting silver as the metal of choice over
gold. In so doing the Hebraic wisdom was sending a message
about idol worship, mastering the materialist impulse to
acquire, time, humility, and the rhythms of life, amongst others. For the Hebraic civilization, time was not to be a quanti-
ty estimated by seconds, minutes, hours, etc. Instead, time
was measured by the waxing and waning of a celestial orb —
the moon — that went through many phases and was a reflection of the sun, in whose shadow it stood, as a humble servant stands in the shadow of his master.

The shift to silver refers as well to the reflected light of
the moon, the silvery moon. The moon is the celestial body
associated with intuition. Moses transmitted the wisdom of
intuition that is the prophetic tradition of Hebraic civiliza-

tion. When the Israelites freed themselves from the yoke of Egyptian oppression, they were, on an inner level, overturning the supremacy of rational, logical thought brought to an exquisite pinnacle in Egyptian architecture, and their development of sacred geometry. The sun and its color yellow mean intellect brought to its highest degree. The moon and its color silver mean emotion — the heart taking the higher position. With the heart becoming paramount, humility assumes a more central position; just as the moon bows to the sun, so the heart bows to the Holy One of highest possible intellect and love. Naturally, when intuition and humility take a central role, and love becomes predominant, we shall find the presence of obedience, poverty, and chastity taken on quite easily: bowing before the Holy One = obedience; love for and from the Holy One = chastity; withdrawing from the intellect to the domain of intuition, from gold to silver = poverty.

We are not to propel ourselves into the spotlight, coaxing others to adore or worship us, to make ourselves a sun. There can only be one sun that stands above us, and above that sun is the supreme Sun, who has created one sun. Judaism, in its deepest wisdom, has asked of us to be like the moon; seek no personal glory, come and go without incident, and don't make material life your goal . . . don't lust after gold.

SAMSON: SYMBOL OF STRENGTH AND REDEMPTION

Samson represents the symbol of strength in life. He had many remarkable qualities, including inhuman strength. He was accorded great stature among his people as a prophet and judge. He was also a "nazir," a righteous man who was a repository of spiritual wisdom. The nazirites were men and women who took on a disciplined practice that included letting the hair grow and not cutting it, for hair in the West has the meaning of strength and sexuality. They also had to abstain from wine or other intoxicants, and to not have contact with a dead body. Samson is amongst this select group mentioned in the Bible, he being the most famous. In fact, he was anointed by his parents while he was in the womb at the behest of God. Even before birth he is bound to the vow of chastity, to the vow of non-intoxication, either sexually, or through substance abuse.

The ongoing story of Samson I shall describe shows a wearing away of his strength and chastity, culminating in his downfall through his liaison with a foreign woman named Delilah. He begins by appearing as the epitome of the warrior, by whose strength the people can be saved from the forces of destruction. This strength can only be used constructively by avoiding excess of the senses and remaining chaste, a clear connection being made here between the two. The vow of chastity is constituted on one level as a prescription for health because it is the primary way to conserve strength and life force. This is why in spiritual life there are strict measures taken pertaining to sexual activity.

For the Western way sexuality is bound up directly to life in terms of its being the vehicle for procreation and love. However, in practice, much sexual activity is done for its own sake to provide sensory gratification without consideration of the partner's experience. Twentieth-century psychology has certainly made a living from this fact. It seems that Samson's story has many parallels to our world of modern psychology. We have been devastated by a spate of sexual plagues in the twentieth century that have been engendered in part by the Freudian psychological movement. Freudianism has been the Philistine equivalent for our time. The legacy of this movement has been to prompt us to open the door to uncontrolled sexuality without guilt. True, this urge was condoned as a response to what was perceived as the repressive sexuality of Victorian, nineteenth-century Europe. Nonetheless, the unintended consequence of this backlash has been a weakening of the moral fiber and moral strength of our society. In its place we are witnessing explosive violence and a disrupted order in life. It is a Philistine life that awaits us if we don't take the steps to preserve our life force. Sexual disturbances abound as much now as they did when Freud began his investigations into the matter.

The fact that sex is more easily talked about today, and is portrayed more freely in the media than ever, doesn't stem the tide of disturbances around this function. All that has happened really in laying bare the "naked truth" about sex from the scientific, iconoclastic side has been that people are having sex more freely at an earlier age for purposes of intoxication than ever before. The upshot of that has been the development of the plague of venereal diseases, culminating with HIV, AIDS, and other retroviral diseases that have laid waste millions and have contributed mightily to the weakened immune systems that characterize much of the chronic disease we see nowadays. (That AIDS is spread in great measure through drugs only underscores the risks and repercussions of seeking intoxication. It also substantiates the necessity for the vow of chastity.)

Samson faced a great challenge inherent, in the nazirite tradition, of remaining chaste despite all temptations. And Delilah was for him the ultimate temptation. We are all subject to temptations endlessly in this life. Like Samson, very few of us are able to resist them. We are pulled into serving other gods, the intoxicant or debauched act becoming an object of worship and idolatry.

Not only is the Second Commandment breached, but the Seventh — adultery — as well. To serve other gods is an act of adultery. Samson committed psychic and carnal adultery. It is very likely that attachment to sexual pleasure will lead to carnal adultery. It is almost inevitable that indulgence leads to promiscuity leads to illicit sexual activity, i.e., adultery, itself the single most destructive factor for family life that we know.

Samson's one weakness was his lust for women. It also happened these women were not of Jewish origin. So, even though he was ordained by the Angel of the Lord to destroy the Philistines, meaning those of impurity who worship false gods, who had ruled over Israel for forty (that number again) years, he still had the choice of choosing to act against God. The inherent freedom to act, to choose life or death, is uniquely human and cannot be removed from us while we are conscious.

Samson is an immensely tragic figure, having enormous gifts that he lets go to waste. His life is absolutely enigmatic because the details of it are so skimpy. In fact, there are no recorded instances of his prophesying or of rendering any act of leading the community, as judges were supposed to do. So, we are hard put to quite understand what happened to him that led him to make such a grave error with Delilah, who herself symbolizes betrayal. One thing we may take as a message from Samson's story is that we must never take anything for granted, especially talents and gifts that are with us from birth. They are the ones we didn't have to work for; they are natural gifts from God. Here, what appear to be our greatest strengths can turn out to be our greatest weakness, particularly when we treat our strengths cavalierly and casually. For this, Samson is our lesson. He allowed himself to sap his strength by dint of the debauched practices in which he engaged. He was too active sexually, especially for one who had a special station in life. He substituted one addiction for another by becoming sexually intoxicated rather than substance intoxicated through alcohol. Of course, any intoxication is against the vow of chastity.

While Samson is with Delilah, she has to find out the source of his strength. She pesters him continuously about this, and he responds by telling her three stories. He fools her each time and is really teasing her. She is undaunted and persists, all the while having sex with him. Finally, he becomes vexed and worn out, and divulges the truth, whereupon he is attacked by the Philistines, who had been lying in wait. They subdue him, gouge out his eyes, and take him into captivity.

Being in a weakened state then made him susceptible to Delilah's imprecations. She was simply a symptom of his downward spiral. It was inevitable that he suffer the fate that befell him.

Unrestrained and immoderate sexuality not only violates chastity, but also deals a blow to the Second and Eighth Commandments. Regarding the second, generally speaking, indulgent sexuality instills a feeling of power and lust, creating a sense of grandiosity and smugness in us that is hard to eliminate. It is clearly recognized in spiritual life that sexual activity has to be highly regulated and used judiciously. It is well known that many spiritual sects practice celibacy. Taoism speaks directly of equating sexual energy with life energy, and how engaging in the former depletes the latter. Conservation of life is intimately connected with conservation of semen for the Taoist. In India, a spiritual practice is done, called Tantra, that is organized around sexual practices where men and women cohabit without reaching climax by withdrawing the secretions back into the body at the point of emission, and using that energy for creative and other life-preserving pursuits. In Judaism, sexual practices are highly regulated and prescribed so that sexuality serves procreation and other forms of creation. In some Kabbalistic practices, sexual impulses serve as a basis for spiritual elevation by turning the lustful experience — called the evil inclination — to the love of God — called the good inclination. Certain masters of this tradition went so far as to say that the greater the lustful impulse, the greater heights the aspirant could reach.

The Eighth Commandment is involved simply because excess sexuality robs ourselves of our life force. Is it not coincidental that athletes are advised not to have sexual activity prior to whatever contest in which they are participating.

* * *

Samson's story evolves into one of redemption and atonement. After he is subdued by the Philistines. Samson is chained, becomes a slave and an object of scorn and ridicule. However, he comes to his senses, realizes his grave error, and seeks to atone for his transgression. Under the very noses of his captors, he regrows his hair. At a public demonstration organized by the Philistines to humiliate him and celebrate the capture of their greatest enemy, three thousand men and women gather, Samson is ordered to dance for them. After doing so, he is left standing between the pillars of the stadium. He prays to God for the strength to destroy his mortal enemies, the ones he was mandated by his birth to destroy, and finds his strength restored. With a cry, "Let me die with the Philistines," he pulls down the pillars, killing more people in death than he had in life.

As it was with Samson, so it is for us all that corrections are always possible for our mistakes. Actually, Samson's redemption, for a figure who was almost literally larger than life, gives us hope that in an "ordinary" life we can find that same possibility for ourselves. We all have the heroic possibility to overcome our enslavement, borne out of our own created errors, and rectify the damage done through/by finding our way back to God.

DAVID AND GOLIATH: FEARLESSNESS

David is one of the most eminent figures of the Bible: a warrior of unparalleled renown; the most important king of the forty-two who ruled over Judah; the psalmist who wrote one of the most significant books of healing ever penned; a healer who used music innovatively to bring peace of mind and relief to his predecessor King Saul, who suffered from manic-depressive illness.

Amongst David's legacy was establishing Jerusalem as the capital of the Jewish people and the center of monotheistic practice, from where the Messiah will come as a direct descendant from David.

David's life is detailed more fully than any other in the Bible. Within this context I have selected two that represent qualities necessary for inner transformation and freedom: David and Goliath and David and Jonathan.

Like Moses, David is prepared for his life mission by having to tend a flock of sheep for forty years. His job was to protect them from harm, rather than not lose any, like Moses. The difference lies in David's role to be played out as the great protector and warrior of the Jews. While tending the flock, he has the occasion to encounter on separate occasions a marauding lion and bear. He engages each directly with his bare hands and kills them. Not using a spear here is meaningful, as it presages his oncoming battle with Goliath, the Philistine giant warrior who threatens the very existence of the Jewish people. Goliath challenges, with all of his weapons, any soldier of the Jewish army to combat, claiming that if he won the Jews would become servants of the Philistines, and if he lost the Philistines would become servants of the Jews. It was here that David came forth bearing only a slingshot, which provoked further taunting by Goliath, who was in full battle regalia. David's stones killed Goliath, whom he beheaded. When the Philistines saw what happened, they fled (not carrying out Goliath's promise) with the Jews in pursuit.

David's encounter with Goliath represents everyman (everywoman) and his battle against the forces that seek to squash our freedom, to oppress us, and to eventually enslave us. Goliath is brute force that operates outside the conventional system of order without conscience.

David is unafraid of the intimidator and confronts him directly. He doesn't shirk nor shrink from defending himself and the community from the "natural born killer" who appears to be every one's nightmare. As part of his spiritual training, which included becoming leader of the Jewish people, he has to demonstrate fearlessness no matter what or how seemingly dire the circumstances. Fear makes us lose our good judgment and brings us into disorder. What made David so fearless? I believe he walked in the way of God.

Goliath is the evil we all face in our everyday life while he is also a reflection of our own impulses — reminiscent of the monsters we grappled with as toddlers and young children that so frequently showed up in our nightmares. We can also note the preoccupation of young children with monsters and the defenders against them, like the Power Rangers. As well, we find the endless fascination with dinosaurs and other prehistoric creatures.

David's slaying of Goliath brings to light an important aspect of healing, namely, homeopathy. When he fought the giant, David succeeded by using a small substance, a stone in a slingshot, to kill him, stating all the while that he was an agent of God, coming in the name of God to conquer the marauder.

In the homeopathic way of healing, an axiom exists identifying a basic principle of this method: a small amount of a substance is all that is needed to bring about a healing response.

This is exactly what David brought to bear against the awesome enemy. As big as Goliath was, that was how small David's remedy needed to be.

The implications of this approach to danger is immense. Applying this idea to disease, a direction of therapeutics suggests, nay, recommends itself. If we take cancer to be an analogous Goliath, it seems that utilizing homeopathic understanding may have benefit. Certainly, this application has been of significance in my clinical practice where I employ homeopathy of the mind called mental imagery to effect healing of Goliath-like illnesses, both physically and emotionally.

Today, in cancer treatment, chemotherapy is given in exactly the opposite way of homeopathy. The doses are given in a military fashion using overwhelming artillery to blow up the enemy. It doesn't work. No Goliath capitulates to force of arms. Using such a method leaves the person's body overwhelmed and unable to mount its own inner strength to help combat this inner Philistine. David recommends instead homeopathy and prayer, a prescription well worth heeding in our struggle with modern-day Goliaths.

David was selected by the prophet Samuel as a replacement for King Saul, the latter having become mentally ill. Saul was picked by Samuel to rule as the children of Israel asked for a king to reign over them, forgetting there was a King already reigning over them. God told Samuel that ever since Egypt, the children of Israel had forgotten their true KING and sought to live in a godless existence. This state of affairs has great historical interest as we see the same situation existing in our own time. We in the modern world have forgotten or denied our KING as ever it was in the time of Samuel three thousand years ago.

In Samuel's day, God decreed that kings should come to rule as a punishment, as people would come under the yoke of a human rule and suffer autocratic strictures imposed on them. God simply put a crimp in the freedom available to us because we asked for it. When we forget God, we surrender our freedom and have to come under the aegis of political and governmental institutions that have not the slightest interest in our securing freedom, or in making life less burdensome for us. In fact, the opposite is the case. There has never been a government that was "of the people, for the people, by the people" in recorded history.

In the mystical Kabbalistic wisdom literature, there is an allusion to our current disorder as it explains the reason for our current imbalance. It is stated there that the earth mirrors the body of God, each part of our world representing a part of the anatomy of God. The heart in this earthly form is Israel. It is to be noted that if the heart is not in order, the rest of the body cannot be in order. The rest of the body depends on the heart's action and the flow of its life giving blood for continued life. It is clear that Israel — the heart — is not in order; order here meaning fulfilling the covenant with God to become "a kingdom of priests and a holy nation" (Exo. 19:6). And, so, the rest of the world has to remain in disorder.

David's odyssey began when he had to elude King Saul, who was envious of him and wanted to kill him. This, in spite of David's efforts at helping Saul overcome his clinical depression, which rendered him mentally unbalanced. David, as creative as he was a warrior, played the lyre to help soothe Saul. This is the first recorded instance of the use of music as a therapeutic intervention to "soothe the savage beast."

When he became king, David fought mightily against all the foreign governments — as well as his own when Saul sought to kill him — and their armies, defeating them all in the name of God to preserve the freedom of the community of the children of Israel. He followed the spiritual injunction that when the tiger comes to kill you, you must respond by killing it first. When David was done being the model of fearlessness and bravery, and being the model for leadership in a world of warfare, murder, and lust for dominance, as has been evidenced in the world's recorded history, he wrote one of the supreme healing texts ever penned — the Psalms, that proclaimed the greatness of God, His overriding importance in the affairs of men, His necessity in our lives when we are sick, fearful, "trembling unto death," and feeling lost in the world.

DAVID AND JONATHAN: UNCONDITIONAL LOVE

David and Jonathan's relationship is often considered the greatest love story in the Bible. Many people unacquainted with biblical wisdom may well wonder why a relationship between two young men, who were not homosexual, should stand above a relationship between a man and a woman, or between two women for that matter, as a model of love.

The answer seems to lie in the realm of the friendship that existed between them. Their bond was deep, everlasting, and united them as one. The character of Jonathan is unparalleled for its humility and honesty. As King Saul's son, he is an heir apparent to the throne of Israel when Saul deceases. However, Jonathan recognizes the greatness of David, and realizes that David is the one who must become king. He does not hesitate for one instant to acknowledge this understanding and campaigns and fights vigorously to save David's life against a raging Saul, who wants desperately to murder David.

Jonathan has no envy, jealousy, or competitiveness toward David, all of which must be absent to truly love. They announce openly their love for each other. It is not homosexual in nature because there is no sexual component involved, this latter erotic element being a requirement in male homosexual relationships. It should also be noted that Jonathan risks his own life to save David's life. It is an axiom of spiritual life that a human being is never to sacrifice himself for another human being. This is so, for to do such is an act of idolatry. This condition does not apply when a person sacrifices himself for the sake of the entire community. Jonathan was acting on behalf of the entire community of Israel, not for David per se.

* * *

Unconditional love is peculiarly human. Other types of love, such as motherly love, brotherly love, or sexual love, are shared by the animal kingdom, and are subject to contingencies and conditions. True love is unconditional, with no contingencies, and no requirement for requital. Jonathan is the epitome of that state. He abandoned his crown in this material world not only for his friend David, but for the entire nation of Israel, for whom David became the necessary monarch who ruled for forty (that number again) years. Jonathan means the one who will give, the giver. David means the beloved. The one who gives without the desire to get is the one who truly loves. Lovingness is, it just exists irrespective of whatever are the circumstances.

To be loved is another matter. One of the great mistakes we make in life is to hitch ourselves to the need to be loved. We have been adversely influenced by twentieth-century psychology to believe that so much disturbance comes from not being loved, and we spend much energy trying to be loved, get love, of pining over not being loved.

We translate this erroneous belief into blaming our parents for not loving us as children, or not loving us enough. And, such a notion has become the bedrock of psychology to the extent that it has sought to controvert the Fifth Commandment to honor father and mother. Our parents have accepted to put us here on earth. This is an incredible blessing because we now have the opportunity to take the decision to find God, to make union with God.

We often believe that we have a right to be loved as a child. To be loved as a child is a privilege in life, not a right. There is no question that a truly loving atmosphere in growing up contributes to a loving nature in adult life. Whatever the conditions are obtaining in early life, it still becomes the task of all of us to become loving and to distance ourselves from the will to power.

There are many conditions that obtain when we need to be loved. Being in this state we will do almost anything to get it. In this circumstance, we may often corrupt ourselves, or make ourselves vulnerable to somebody else's power, which may manifest as withholding, abusive, sadistic, toying, ignoring, taking for granted, etc. Whenever we need to be loved, there is *always* a condition that has to be met, either by what we demand from the other person, or in turn is demanded from us. And, the condition(s) is rarely, if ever, met. Jonathan needs nothing in return. His way is the model for how love has to impact itself on the world. Jonathan gives up pride in the wake of love. Pride is a breaking of the Second Commandment and is one of the greatest impediments to harmony between people that we know in life. It is the defense of vanity, the false picture we paint of ourselves as being important or special.

Jonathan conveys the spiritual message of impoverishing oneself to fame, wealth, and power, for a higher reward in God's world. The vow of poverty is lived out through him. He follows the Tenth Commandment as well of not coveting.

Jonathan, in giving up the crown, exemplifies the vow of poverty, absenting himself from the riches and power such investiture would create. He gives up the riches of this world for a reward that no amount of money can buy, that of the crown of heaven. He is one of the three people of the Bible who surrenders material reward for the riches bestowed by heaven.

So, Jonathan is a model of how to achieve peace on this earth. With all the chaos existing here, we all have the possibility for union simply by making that decision. Were a critical mass — roughly five percent of the world's population to make that decision, the consciousness and conscience of this world would shift dramatically to a world of love, peace, and brotherhood.

Love is a theme the Biblical sages did not focus on in an extensive way as was done by the followers of Jesus, who were forming the offshoot of Judaism called Christianity. The Biblical masters were well aware of love's strength and necessity, as witnessed by the great paean to love penned by David's son Solomon, called The Song of Songs. Here Solomon proclaims his great love for God, whom he likens to a magnificently beautiful woman. In this epic work he said, "love is strong as death" (Song 8:6). The implications of that statement are quite powerful and is for the final chapter of my last book, *Healing Into Immortality,* where I proposed that the core aim of Western spirituality — the overcoming of death — and love as the vital force making that happen.

* * *

Other biblical statements are quite clear and distinct about love: love God with all your heart, with all your soul, with all your might (Deut. 6:5); love your neighbor as yourself (Lev. 19:18). These statements say it all, their ramifications profound and go to the heart of the meaning and purpose for living in this world bereft of God's presence. The essence of these statements simply says, "Don't have any conditions entering into your lovingness. Be unconditional in your love feelings." Love!

Jonah and the Whale: Compassion, Atonement

Jonah and the Whale is a story about obedience, compassion, and atonement. It holds a special place in the wisdom literature in that it is recited at the time of Yom Kippur, the Day of Atonement, perhaps the single holiest day of the year for Jews.

Jonah is a prophet who is summoned by God to go to Nineveh to tell the people there to mend their "violent and evil ways," or that God would destroy that city. Jonah does not want to follow out this command because he does not like the Ninevehites and would prefer to see them perish. He sets out to avoid God by heading out to sea as a passenger in a fisherman's boat manned by a crew. God creates an enormous storm that frightens the crew and makes them fear for their lives. Jonah realizes what has happened and tells the crew to send him overboard so they can be saved. They do so and he is swallowed by a whale, in whose belly he resides for three days. During this interment he repents and seeks forgiveness for his disobedience. At the end of that time he is disgorged by the whale on the shore by the city of Nineveh, precisely the place he was trying to avoid. He does go and preach to them as God has ordered, and they repent. Jonah is still not happy about having had to speak to a people he did not care for. He goes and sits on a hillside overlooking the city, still not certain, after his ordeal, that he wants to follow God's order. God covers Jonah at night with a large gourd to protect him from the elements. Jonah is thankful. When he wakes in the morning he finds the gourd eaten by worms.

The sun then beats down mercilessly on Jonah's head together with a violent east wind, and he fainted. When he awoke he begins to cry for the gourd being destroyed. God asked Jonah if he was angry about the gourd. Jonah said he was so angry that he wanted to die because the gourd withered, and he was sad. God gently chides him by pointing out to Jonah that he had pity on the gourd which Jonah didn't make to grow or labored to create and which lived and died in one day, so why shouldn't God have pity on the inhabitants of Nineveh who are ignorant and are like cattle? He was giving Jonah an important lesson about judging people from a human perspective which no human has the right to do. We may hold people accountable for their acts without judgment, aware that no one is exempt from the cosmic law of needing to pay consequences for actions. By the same token, the ignorant ones, whether they be acting inadvertently, knowingly, or maliciously, must be educated; otherwise they will never learn and the cycle of needless suffering has to continue on the earth.

It is the responsibility of those who know about Spirit to teach those who don't know. The indifferent ones may have their cold heart melt through education. The knowers of Spirit do try to reach everyone, and are not discouraged by indifference . . . or depravity.

For the callous ones, educative methods cannot be done by words but by actions. That is they have to be made to feel what it is they are doing, by having it done to them, and under no circumstances appeasing them. Doing to them what they are doing is a homeopathic application of healing, which states that "like cures like," and fulfills the ancient maxim "Don't do unto others what you wouldn't have them to do unto you" (Lev. 19:18). Words for the indifferent souls work in the dark. Unfortunately, the numbers of indifferent people in the world are legion, and are growing by leaps and bounds.

Why? One reason is TV! The violent messages passed through TV are numbing and inure people to violence, making it an acceptable way of life. It also passes along a message to the brutal that their acts are not only tacitly acceptable but will gain them notoriety as media events. This callousness has even crept into the Walt Disney films for children. They are violent, show harsh, unloving behavior between characters, and use offensive language all coated over by cutesy cartoon characters. Another avenue for teaching violence is the ever-present rap music, heavy metal music, and other forms of rock music that pass along suggestions to carry out violent behavior and to hate, encoded in the hypnotic backgrounds of the beats. As has been documented, when this music is played in reverse there are often encoded violent messages. This has been the subject of a number of recent law cases brought against record companies whose lyrics contain the subliminal messages that have led to suicide attempts by unwary teenage listeners.

* * *

Another aspect of what God teaches Jonah is how we can relate to anger, how to replace anger with compassion and the efficacy of prayer bringing about healing. Jonah is angry that he is called upon to deliver a message to a group of people whom he judged to be wicked and for whom he felt should be punished. He becomes angry with God for not punishing them because he deemed it necessary they be punished. God shows him by a very clever maneuver of the gourd how to analogize the pain he felt about the gourd's destruction to the destruction of a large number of people so that he would feel compassion for those whom God spared.

God demonstrated to Jonah that an entire population can save itself from destruction by acts of repentance and atonement. God said in effect, "Don't worry! There is still hope for humanity. Let them know what they are doing and that they are going to demise in forty (that number again) days. Giving them a shock will stimulate them to take a new action, one of repentance and repair." This is a clear message for modern Western society, which is suffering from plagues of illness, violence, and deterioration threatening its very existence. There is no question but to pay for its misdeeds of the past and present for the exploitation of the peoples of the world. Part of atonement concerns making active corrections and compensations to those who have been injured. The greed factor and the will to power combine to render us blind to this universal law of payment.

It has been the aim of Monotheistic life to teach atonement and repentance, which are needed to help tame the murderous, destructive impulses abounding in the world.

Like Jonah, each of us on the path of Spirit is mandated to speak about Exodus to everyone; we are mandated to alert the populace about their irresponsible murderous behavior; we are mandated to be a "light to the nations" (Isa. 42:6), to cast out the darkness that envelops the human condition. In the Monotheistic spiritual tradition, we are supposed to fight this evil, not appease or run from it. According to Exodus, if each of us does not set the example, nobody will.

Jonah was the reluctant prophet who wanted not to show mercy — also known as lovingkindness — on the evildoers. But, the prophets had a mission to bear God's message throughout the land and not question the whys and wherefores of that mission. The analogies of what was going on in Nineveh to our contemporary situation are startling. Even Jonah's being swallowed by a leviathan analogizes to our current relationship to the computer age and the artifactual term called "cyberspace" that is creating a frenzied pace to our rhythm of life that is impossible to adapt to and remain balanced. Jonah prays for deliverance from the clutches of this monster and agrees to take the spiritual message to the people. God, in an act of love, delivers Jonah from the whale's belly. So strong is God that even the crew of the ship that bore Jonah away from Nineveh recognized the supremacy of this One over their own gods so that they prayed to One for help against the raging sea.

There is a parallel theme of atonement in Jonah's story. He atones twice. One he does when he confesses to the crew that he is the cause of the travail they face and he offers himself up to the sea to save the crew and ship from destruction. Again, when he is in the body of the whale he atones for defying God's command and after three days, he is inscribed for life. Then, he makes the trip to Nineveh over a three-day period where he tells them they have forty days to change their ways.

In Jonah's story we see the numbers three and ten appear often. In the esoteric Western wisdom, the number three (Jonah's time in the whale) has the meaning of the synthesis of possibilities. It brings into unity the natural oppositions that stand at the foundation of the dual world in which we live. In life our existence is based on the inherent knowledge of opposites. For example, when you look outside and say that it is daytime, you cannot possibly enunciate nor articulate this fact unless you understand the existence of night. All that we know, feel, and do has to do with the existence of opposites. If you deem yourself to be an active person, you couldn't know that unless you understood passive. If you want to be important it's because you understand and are avoiding inferiority.

In the spiritual practice of the Three Vows and Ten Commandments, what transpires is that these oppositions are not seen as adversarial to one another, but rather can be appreciated as being authentic aspects of life, and genuine parts of our existence. For example, things are not good or bad, right or wrong, but good and bad, right and wrong, without critical judgment. By including everything rather than excluding or rejecting one side of the matter as "bad" or as an "enemy," they can come together in a union that produces a third possibility inclusive of the other two, but is different from them and transcends them, while bringing us at the same time to a new level of personal evolution, a new synthesis.

Synthesis means an organic development from within stemming from the unbiased and unprejudiced acceptance of whatever exists in this world. It is tantamount to following the biblical appeal to say "yes to life" (Deut. 30:19), accept all without judgment and without the need to provide an opinion or story about your perception.

Take the lived experience of fear, for instance. The opposite of fear is excitement, or fearlessness. You may recoil in fear and recoil from fearlessness when faced with a situation calling for it. Without judging yourself harshly for being fearful, accept it as an authentic response to life. Each instance of fear calls for being excited or fearless. If you can't be fearless in the situation, accept it without self-condemnation.

Opening to these possibilities brings you to a place of equanimity and balance that transcends these opposites and brings an experience of relaxation and moving forward rather than away from encountering and tasting of the possibilities this world offers. We become enriched in the process, and interestingly, we will develop a sense of detachment about what was formerly important to us. Practicing detachment brings us closer to a state of detachment that is so necessary to engage in the process of chastity and poverty. Detachment is not to be confused with indifference. The latter is a state of uncaring and callousness; the heart is cold. In detachment we are in exactly the reverse state: caring, warm, heartfelt. The number three speaks to detachment and raising ourselves above the coils of the serpent.

So, the Ninevehites are given a test of forty days to detach from their "violent, evil ways." And they do so through a communal act of atonement, by donning sackcloth and ashes and bowing down before God in an act of mass humility. In essence, the act of atonement consists of taking the Three Vows.

Jonah is shown the errors of his ways and he responds by atoning. The same thing happens with the larger group of Nineveh. It is no wonder that this story occupies a central place on the Day of Atonement.

We are the citizens of Nineveh who have to atone for the errors of our ways. The time is rapidly coming, as we become aware of the analogy to our life now, that sackcloth and ashes will become the order of the day. That day can't approach soon enough. It is coming, and it is wonderful that it is. We are getting to the forty-day period. Like the people of Nineveh we have created the need for it to happen. It has become a natural progression, since the Vietnam War, of the creation of the possibility of ending world wars. Consequently, we have encountered for the first time in American history, and perhaps in all of Western Europe as well, a generation that will not be engaged in turning its aggressive and murderous impulses, conditioned over the centuries by endless wars, outward toward an external enemy. As a result, this collective energy has nowhere to go but implosively into American life, with Americans fighting Americans, assaulting each other, killing each other, wreaking violence against each other in alarming degrees. We have not had to face a phenomenon like this on our own soil since the Civil War, but the magnitude and complexities of the issues are far beyond those of the Civil War and at the same time an extension of the issues surrounding that conflict.

One of the beauties of the story of Jonah is how destiny and free will are intimately tied to one another. He cannot escape his destiny as much he tries to by dint of exercising his free will to say "no" to God. By destiny, I mean direction, not fate. Fate implies chance, and within the precincts of spiritual understanding, there is no chance. Everything is within Divine Providence, and has a meaning, although we may not be able to glean the meaning easily. There is a divine cosmic plan guiding the destiny of this earth, and universe, within which we humans, being the limitless creatures we are, have the freedom of God imbued and imprinted in us. This is the most important paradox, I believe, we have to embrace. Essentially, the basis of the divine plan is the inexorable movement toward eternal life. We can choose to align our-selves with this life plan or can opt out and be in the move-ment toward death. This is the great challenge in human life: how are we to use our God-given free will? Do we give it away to the serpent, as Adam and Eve did in Eden, or do we rightfully thank God for the gift of freedom He has given us? Do we obey the gift-giver or remain unruly children? The answer remains to be seen.

JOB: OBEDIENCE, PATIENCE

The story of Job is one of many men, because many appar-ently righteous people have unaccountably, and seemingly undeserved, afflictions happening to them. The Jobian indi-vidual is one who suffers deprivation and loss and has to withstand the test of involuntary impoverishment without losing faith in God while undergoing the test of good versus evil.

In the battle of Good versus Evil, which is the essential element of the Western spiritual tradition, we are all the play-ers on that great stage as the mystical bard William Shake-speare so eloquently put it. In the moral tradition, standing as it does as the foundational point of Western mysticism, there is an absolute necessity for the existence of good and evil. This dualism has to be present when we posit a moral world, as morality implies that we act either for the purpose of sus-taining the morally preservative, life-affirming direction of life, or for serving the destructive, immorally, life-negating direction of death.

The story starts in the heavenly court where God and his favorite angel Satan are discussing one of God's servants, Job, an unusually pious and generous man. Satan claims that if Job's blessings were removed, he would lose faith in God. God and Satan wager on Satan's assertion. God allows Satan to intervene in Job's life to test Job's piety. Satan destroys Job's wealth, kills his ten children, and afflicts him with painful boils all over his body. Job's three "friends" assume that Job has sinned, for which he is being punished. They urge him to repent. Job insists he has not sinned and that he is willing to accept all that God gives, including the evil, but avers that this change in fortune does not mean that he is guilty of sinning.

Job was the man of utter faith and patience who prevailed in the face of shock after shock after shock without experiencing a "post-traumatic stress" disturbance. Within the context of all the losses he suffered, he also discovered who his friends were. He finds out, as most of us have, that who we thought were friends are really false comforters who did not have our best interests at heart. What is generally revealed in times of travail is really how disloyal, jealous, and envious so-called friends can be. This has been my personal experience, as well as what I have encountered everywhere I look; and I have seen so often in patients with cancer where supposed friends desert the sufferer, much to the latter's dismay and shock. I may say also that in my clinical practice I have seen the benefit reaped by these same cancer patients when they find these purported friends leaving them. Cancer is one of the best weeding-out processes I have seen. In the overwhelming majority of instances, those afflicted have found it beneficial in the long run to have gained the knowledge of what is true friendship.

* * *

Job exemplifies the vow of chastity. He remains forever faithful to God despite all the horrendous events befalling him. His message simply is: no matter what happens to you, whether you regard it as "good or "bad," it all is a part of God's plan that includes that we all need to gain something from everything happening to us so that we can become free of illusion, find out what we have to master in ourselves, and learn what is our purpose for being here on earth. Becoming free, self-mastery, our purpose for being are all acts of discovery that come from making a search in this direction.

I can certainly write that our purpose on earth is to find God. I know this is a truth about our existence, but such a statement has to remain an intellectual abstraction until you can discover that truth for yourself. Job, I believe, thought he had found God until he was put to the test. That is, he had to understand that there was more to go than what he might have settled for in his connection with God. Isn't it so that when everything is going well, we praise God for our good fortune, but when adversity strikes we immediately turn our backs on God, revile Him, blame Him, and become angry with Him for letting it happen to us? Losing faith is easily experienced when things haven't gone our way. God is blamed for abandoning us. This attitude has prevailed throughout history and has left many people feeling agnostic, atheistic, or apostatic (deserting of faith). Not so Job. Regardless of what happened and how much the false comforters who visited him after the catastrophes, fobbing themselves off as friends, who accused him unjustly of impiety, he never wavered in his belief that whether it be good times or bad times, never falter in your faith in God. This faith is all that matters, not the prevailing circumstances of the moment.

Job historically represents the history of those people who have had to endure endless attempts at exterminating them, which persists to this day. Job's tests came as a spiritual one akin to what Adam and Eve experienced in the garden. His test came from above, from the heavenly realm, not from his own created errors. He had evolved to a high level of self-mastery and now the "angels of the left," the prosecutorial angels, with permission of God, decided to throw a test his way. Yes, while it is so that most of what happens to us is of our making, there are instances, like Job, Adam and Eve, Abraham and Isaac, where the tests are not of our making but come from "above."

The angels of the left are constantly looking for convictions on the human level, convinced as they are that we have sinned, transgressed, and have committed iniquities. As these angels of the left are considered to be at left of God, i.e., cast out of the heavenly court, they are considered to be agents of evil. It should be understood, contrary to all organized church teachings, that evil never wants to interfere with the freedom of the individual. It comes as a test to the individual, and to the larger community as well, to help move us to the next level in our personal development.

Most of us, however, are dealing with our own man-made demons. The artificial demons are those constructed through the agency of our own thought process and distressing emotional experiences. When we become anxious or worried, for example, or concoct stories about some anticipated future occurrence that hasn't happened yet, and therefore, cannot be true, then we have created a mental child. Once created, this mental child becomes an autonomous creature making all the demands that a physical child does. It demands to be fed, nurtured, given attention, and to have its orders carried out. It siphons off our energy and we end up doing its bidding. It is as though this artificially constructed Frankenstein becomes the monster/demon that takes possession of us and enslaves us. Job demonstrated none of these traits. He was able to remain centered in the presence of all these calamities. By remaining faithful to God, he does not fall prey to those manmade artificial demons.

People have asked me as to how we are to distinguish these tests from what we have created for ourselves. An answer to that is that you know instinctively. You don't feel guilt. You can assess the situation and cannot find where you have sinned, transgressed, or have erred maliciously. You may even consult a trusted spiritual friend for objective eyes to confirm your perspective. Furthermore, in these situations, you find that even though you may experience physical and mental pain, your mood does not falter and can still maintain a cheerful or equanimous disposition. There is always "God answering Job out of the whirlwind" (Job 38:1) that those who maintain faith always manage to hear the voice of truth amidst all the cacophony abounding in this world.

Almost the entirety of the noise emitted in the world has no truth value connected with it, but it does have enormous volume, so much so that it drowns out that inner voice, the intuitive voice, that comes as a gut feeling or heartfelt sense that provides us with all the knowledge we need. What Job did was to shun the outside noise in the guise of the false comforters who came to revile him. He was not swayed for one moment by their commentary and maintained his own authority. He passed the test! We are all put to the same test, as we are all Job. We all have to face whether to succumb to outside authorities or to become and maintain our own authority. If we don't become our own authority, we are doomed to a life of enslavement with all its accompanying tortures and suffering.

Job bore very important qualities that made it possible to sustain the misfortunes that befell him. Chief amongst these characteristics were: patience, faith, ability to suffer. By suffer I mean the ability to bear.

First Job had to suffer the losses that all hit him at once. You may make note of this because it commonly happens that when we sustain a loss, it often occurs in/as a cluster, a number of them coming at one time or within a short time of each other. Then he had to manifest patience, the ability to wait while the false comforters were denouncing him. He didn't respond abruptly or impatiently, but was indeed quite rational, sober, and measured.

Finally, he never lost trust in God and his attunement to

All Infinite Being, whom he was quite sure would never let him down or desert him. His faith was duly rewarded at the end of the story, when almost all was restored to him, including many, many long years of life. Interestingly, what wasn't restored was his health, which remained impaired, and in spite of which he lived an additional 145 years. This is an important lesson for all of us regarding our attitude toward ill health: don't panic or cave in in front of illness. We can live very long lives regardless of physical impairment.

NAOMI AND RUTH: LOYALTY

Naomi and Ruth stand as a model for all relationships that prevail harmoniously in a family setting. They represent the ideal relationship to which everyone should aspire. That such a relationship existed is miraculous in itself, and there is much to learn here.

Elimelech, his wife Naomi, and their two sons emigrate to Moab during a famine in their homeland. The two sons marry Moabite women — Ruth and Orpah — and live there ten years. It is there that the two men die. Naomi then blesses the daughters-in-law and urges them to return to their families and remarry, while she returns to her homeland. Orpah follows her advice. But Ruth wants only to go with Naomi and utters the now famous line: "Whither thou goest, I will go. . . . Thy people shall be my people, and thy God, my God." After they arrive in Israel, Ruth is put in touch by Naomi with her cousin Boaz. She guides Ruth's way to win Boaz's heart, and they eventually marry. David is a descendant of that nuptial. Boaz was known as the greatest sage of his generation, his name meaning "in him there is strength."

That Naomi's two Jewish sons married non-Jewish women speaks to, in modern times, a significantly common occurrence in America, where intermarriage is frequent. In the story, the wives take on the religion of Judaism, but they do not convert to the Jewish religion. When Naomi's sons die, and she asks the two women, Ruth and Orpah, to return to the land of the Moabites from which they originally came, Naomi realizes that it may be to the widows' benefit to be amongst their original kinsmen rather than mixing amongst strangers, having to navigate amidst people who, without their husbands to protect them, might have encountered rejection and, perhaps, downright hostility. Naomi didn't want her daughters-in-law to undergo unnecessary hardship. Now, this is a mother-in-law of all mothers-in-law.

Naomi was the manifestation of the balanced individual free of ego concerns, and has to be regarded as one of the most righteous people described in the Bible. She was neither egoistic, egotistic, ego-centered. By ego I mean self-referential (egoistic), self-importance (egotistic), and grandiose self-centeredness (egocentric). She was not envious, jealous, murderous, thieving, or lying. She was the female counterpart of Job and who followed the Deuteronomic injunction to "choose life." There was not a death-oriented impulse in her character. She was indeed mirrored by her daughter-in-law Ruth. Ruth so loves her mother-in-law that she cannot bear the thought of leaving her, no matter what or how arduous the circumstances. She does not hesitate to convert and follow Naomi, and also to heed Naomi's counsel of how to remarry within the family line that is so important to the issue of lineage in Biblical times. Preserving the lineage is an element of following the law of chastity by not mixing, perhaps impure genetic elements from unknown family lines. To maintain family purity is equivalent to maintaining chastity.

That same impulse guiding our ancestors has the same relevance now. The idea then was to keep the gene pool and, therefore, the family physically strong while avoiding the problem of genetic inbreeding that would bring with it genetic defects, diluting and severely weakening the gene pool of the family.

One of the physical illnesses that commonly happens by mixing either by committing adultery or seeking sexual intoxication is venereal disease, which has swept through the world sparing no race over the course of recorded history. A cousin of these diseases is tuberculosis and its ancient distant relative leprosy, mentioned at length in the Bible. My teacher Mme. Colette Aboulker-Muscat pointed out to me a number of years ago that it would be a common finding in people with chronic disease to discover a history of venereal disease and/or T.B. in that individual or in the family line of that individual. I naturally checked out this incredible insight and found that in the overwhelming majority of the patients, this historical reality was verified. The relevance of this finding has great bearing on our clinical work of imagery because we use this finding to use special imagery exercises to clean out this vector and thereby favorably influence the disease being worked on.

We might say that Naomi's story is aligned with that of Job. They both suffer enormous losses one upon the other. Job led a "cushy" life. He was very wealthy, wanting for nothing. Naomi had very little. Yet, in spite of her sparse material life she was *always* happy, never resentful nor complaining. She had none of what we call the intimidating and threatening false selves that try to manipulate the world to do their bidding by complaining, blaming, and standing up for their supposed rights that everything has to come to us on this earth by entitlement rather than earned by merit of one's own good works. In short, she was mature, accepted her place in the world at that immediate moment, was free of ego (or false selves), and *had a relationship with God.* She had what material life cannot buy. She received the blessing of peace of mind and clarity of vision reserved for those who have trod the path of climbing the ladder of self-mastery to reach toward Spirit. She demonstrated this latter quality when she counseled Ruth as to how to win Boaz's heart, the strong Jewish leader with whom she falls in love. This is one of the great spiritual messages of Naomi and Ruth's story: the way for women to behave and comport themselves to find their way to a man's heart. Ruth, as the marvelous student that she was, listened unquestioningly to Naomi's advice and so succeeded.

Ruth's behavior vis à vis Naomi is important in terms of portraying the relationship of the seeker of Spirit to the Master. Ruth recognizes Naomi's greatness and passes the very first test early on, when she responds to Naomi's suggestion to leave with: "whither thou goest I shall go" (Ruth 1:16). As a non-Jew she is impelled to convert when she realizes that the moral and spiritual way of Monotheism contains the direction to follow, so as to live out the Master of Christianity's proclamation to bring peace on earth and goodwill toward our fellow man. Naomi, in the tradition of the spiritual masters of the West, gives Ruth an obstacle to overcome by telling her to return to her own people. Unlike Orpah, who is not yet ready for spiritual practice, Ruth insists on going with Naomi, as the true student has to respond.

Ruth's story is one of spiritual ascent. She is as morally pure as her teacher Naomi, her name meaning pity. She is a woman of great compassion who is on the path to finding God. Her test is to make union with Boaz, the master of strength, to find her own inner strength and embrace her own male energy.

In light of Naomi's high evolutionary development, we might also take note that her name means "pleasant," the meaning of the term *placebo*, a most significant element for healing. To be pleasant requires that we not personalize everything that happens to us, nor personalize everything that we encounter, and not take life so seriously. I might make one comment about this last point. It really is not possible to be lighthearted about life when our thoughts and actions go in the direction of committing errors and of transgressing the commandments.

With respect to this above comment you will almost *never,* for example, see a humorous criminal. They are probably the most serious individuals you will ever meet. Their seriousness is part of their intimidating false selves who act in a threatening way to control the world around them, so they may be able to fulfill the — perhaps by now familiar to you — most influential false belief generally governing life on earth: the purpose of living being to gain pleasure and live in a non-disturbed state, while avoiding pain.

I use the example of the criminal because of the prevalence of this behavior in an open and also tacitly accepted way in Western life at present, where criminals are apotheosized in the media and in film. But the starkness of their character and savagery of behavior betrays an inner life that is far from tranquil and non-disturbed. They display to the extreme what is present in most people's inner life, not to mention manifested in the outer life. The criminal's inhuman coldbloodedness is only an extreme of what most of us are consigned to experience when we live a life apart from God. It is impossible to feel pleasant when not in the orbit of God's love, as was Naomi.

Naomi was simplicity personified; a person who lived the vows of poverty, chastity, and obedience that blended together to create her humility of which simplicity is a hallmark. All of those qualities she imparts to Ruth, who in turn lies humbly at the feet of Boaz, the master of his evil inclinations. Naomi teaches Ruth how to pray, and to take action properly with intention that places her in the service of God. To be a servant of God is the most thrilling occupation on earth. Really, everything else offered in this hedonistically oriented pagan world is in the long run thoroughly boring by contrast. The will to power is basically boring, as is indulging the senses, which is extinguished rather quickly and requires the next more exquisite immediate gratification, otherwise life becomes empty, meaningless, and felt as boring.

One of the greatest fears we all suffer is that of looking squarely into the face of the life of gratification of the senses to realize how vacuous it all is, and that we have sold our soul for a bowl of porridge, while abdicating our creative and spiritual essence. It is worth looking directly into the teeth of this demon because it's the truth. And, while the truth hurts (thankfully), it is, nevertheless, the best medicine. Once recognized, this truth allows us to stop searching in vain for such things as the "seven spiritual laws for achieving success," the subject of a recent popular book. Instead, we can begin looking for the seven laws for attaining *spiritual* success. The point is not to become rich materially, but to become rich spiritually.

Naomi and Ruth represent one of the only, if not the only biblical narratives (perhaps Esther may be another) where the protagonists are free of moral error. The significance here is that it is possible to attain this state of being, and then be in a position to receive the benedictions and grace from above. Interestingly, in contrast to Job, there is no mention of either Naomi or Ruth dying. In fact, the story ends with Ruth giving birth to Obed, the future father of Jesse, the future father of David, who is the great restorer to life of the Hebrew nation and for whom Christianity holds in reverence as the lineage out of which Jesus the Christ came, who bore with him the message of resurrection — the defeat of death.

ESTHER: THE STORY OF TRUTH
AND SELF-REDEMPTION

The story of Esther is one of truth, great presence of mind in the face of the threat of extinction, and of the artful nature of fighting evil. It is a timeless tale, as relevant today as it was those thousands of years ago when it took place.

Esther, as a beautiful Jewish woman, lives in the land of Persia and becomes Queen by outmarrying with Xerxes the king. He has already divorced his wife Vashti. Esther's teacher is her uncle Mordecai, in keeping with Sephardic Jewish tradition where family members are spiritual teachers and pass esoteric transmission from generation to generation.

Esther first catches Xerxes' eye when she wins a beauty contest, while keeping her Jewish origins secret. Shortly after the marriage, Mordecai angers Haman, Xerxes' secretary of state, by not bowing down before him as he passes by in a procession. In Haman's megalomanic rage, he implores Xerxes to issue an edict to exterminate all Jews in the kingdom. He uses the phraseology that has fueled all anti-Semitic propaganda and persecutions in history up to and including the modern day: "There is a certain people, scattered and dispersed among the other peoples in all the provinces of your realm, whose laws are different from those of any other people and who so not obey the king's law, and it is not in your majesty's interests to tolerate them."[6]

The book of Esther tells of the existence of all the Hamans who have ever existed past, present, and future, who have sought the extinction of all the people who follow the way of one God, and all other people deemed "undesirable" by those men of evil who have been with us from Haman to Assiburnipal the Assyrian, Torquemada, the Grand Inquisitor of Spain, Hitler, and Stalin.

It has been noted in Jewish mystical circles that at the time of the coming shift in consciousness known as the "End

of Days," only the holiday Purim, celebrating the story of
Queen Esther will remain, as it relates in its content the
redemption of the world. Because of Esther, the world of
truth and God is saved from the force of evil and destruction.

Mordecai knows he must fight to save the Jews, and tells
Esther to intercede on behalf of her people. She at first refuses: she wants her identity concealed, and besides, the king
hasn't summoned her, she could lose her life for going to
Xerxes without being summoned (a capital crime then).
Mordecai points out to her that she would be naive to think
that in the long run she would survive, and that her identity
would ultimately be ferreted out and she would be killed
anyway.

She finally comes to realize that uncle Mordecai was
right and that she has a mission to fulfill that speaks to and
brings out her inner beauty as well as the outer. She goes to
Xerxes and informs him of the plot and reveals her Jewish
heritage. As a consequence of her action, Haman is hung
instead of Mordecai, and Xerxes sees to it that his Jewish
subjects are fully armed to defend themselves against, and to
destroy their enemies whom Haman set against them before
he died.

There was a precedent about Esther's truthfulness concerning her relationship with her husband. Early on Uncle
Mordecai tells Esther of a plot he uncovered where two advis-
ers to the king were seeking to kill him. Esther is informed by
Mordecai. She in turn tells Xerxes, who takes the necessary
steps to get rid of the intended perpetrators. He then inquires
of Esther as to how she had such knowledge. Her response is:
"[A]nd Esther told the king thereof in Mordecai's name"
(Esth. 2:).

With these words we are led into an understanding of
the depths of human existence. The four levels of knowledge
almost leap out at me as I recount the story.

The literal/historical tells the story of the dangers posed

to believers in truth at any price, the followers of Monotheism who risk their very lives to follow the path of moral greatness. Remember that Mordecai refuses to bow down before Haman. Consequently, Haman, in his madness, becomes enraged and turns his wrath not only to destroy Mordecai, but to the entirety of the Jewish population of the kingdom. Any minority is at risk in a world so dysfunctional as ours, and with such hatred abounding, witness Rwanda and Yugoslavia. The book of Esther is a "so what else is new" story. Thus was it ever so. But, there is a way out embedded in the biblical text in the words of Esther noted above. Let us first look at the other levels.

The moral level is pretty clear. Haman seeks to sacrifice by genocide for the purposes of fulfilling his own megalomanic agenda. Megalomania is the most exaggerated and irreversible form of self-absorption whose aim is to become God and have others bow down before one. To this end, Haman resorts to the "big lie," as Hitler termed it, to remove his enemies by deception, deceit, and despotism from his midst. We have seen a similar scenario played out in Bosnia, where an "ethnic cleansing" was proposed and attempted to be fulfilled. I think it easy to see the dire consequences of taking the moral low road. Thankfully, as was the case of Haman, who was hung, the megalomaniacs eventually come to ruin and we are left to clean up the mess, pick ourselves up, dust ourselves off, and start all over again.

What is the allegory or analogy being pointed to? It is that of the triumph of good versus evil. This is the struggle that permeates our individual and collective lives. When we come before our heavenly King we must appear in truth to be spared. Those nine words uttered by Esther signified to the king the worth and integrity of Esther. She came in humility. She warned the king of danger. She was not a tattle-tale but acting as a servant for a greater good, i.e., to serve the cause of preserving life. She won the king's heart, not through her outer beauty, but through her inner beauty. Little did she know or contemplate what lay ahead. But, she did lay the groundwork for winning the king's trust and confidence when, again, she had to apprise him of great danger.

In the esoteric dimension there is no greater quality that brings us nearer to the King than truth. It is a special quality that quickly takes hold of Esther's character, that makes her one of the most unusual figures in all the legends and mythologies of Western life. Her transfiguration takes place under the tutelage of her teacher, her uncle Mordecai. He deftly brings out of her what is inherently there — fearlessness to confront the terrorists of our lives as an agent of/for truth. Just as King Solomon said that love is strong as death, so it is that truth is strong as evil.

Mordecai is a masterful teacher. He shows strength in the face of intimidation, clarity of perception that allows him to grasp the essential nature of a situation, and an ability to direct someone toward truth without treading on the other's freedom. Esther is quite cognizant of the model of an enlightened master to whom she has surrendered her ego to become a heroine for the sake of the community and not to ask for personal glory.

By answering in truth she convinces Ahasuerus (Xerxes) of her moral integrity. She takes no credit for herself. Instead, she gives credit to her source. Likewise, if we are not able to give credit to our Source, there is no hope for the redemption of this world. This is esoteric talk now. The salvation of the world rests on our ability and willingness to follow God's request made in Eden, and later reiterated with Abraham, that we listen only to His voice. We are not to make the *fundamental* error of wanting to be God. This latter desire has led us down a path of unprecedented death and destruction, creating finally the crisis of possible planetary extinction we now face. The way back from this brink resides with Esther in the nine words of humility and obeisance to a greater authority. She of course does not bow to Mordecai as he is another human. We must never do that. Instead, she venerates him, not worships him. But, she clearly has in mind the yearning to bow before the Almighty King. I'm sure of this because I have this desire as I write these words about Esther.

Those nine words bring into alignment the four levels I've just described. In the esoteric wisdom there are three qualities of character that must be followed: always to be cheerful, never to humiliate someone in public, and to always give credit to your sources. All these entail devotion to God in an environment and atmosphere of humility. To be sad is to forget God and commit self-murder. To humiliate is to sit in judgment of another human, as though we would be God. To not give credit is to mistake oneself for God. This act leads us to believe we are above law and are exempt from cosmic law regarding our thoughts, feelings, and behavior. As we say in Brooklyn, "fuhgeddaboudit."

Esther's statement has given us the key to triumphing over evil and to fulfilling our purpose on earth as God gave to Abraham (Gen. 12:1-3). Please take note that it was a woman who bore the most important message ever delivered to humanity in our recorded history. This fact is to make mention of the importance and significance the place of women has in Western spirituality. Without women like Esther (and many more described in the Bible — like Rebecca), the possibility for the perpetuation of the law of God, and the perpetuation of the life of Monotheism, could not happen. It is truly so affirmed in Western spirituality that the woman is the teacher of the man. To be a teacher in spiritual life is to show us our habitual errors and the ways to correct them.

Out of this story develops one of the most important of Jewish festival days, called Purim. The Hebrew word *pur* means "lot," as in casting lots. When Haman had the decree signed, his minions cast lots to discover on what precise day the edict would be carried out. Hence, the holiday of lots, or Purim is to commemorate the victory of good over evil, and to remind everyone of the ongoing scourge of anti-Semitism and of genocide that lives from generation to generation throughout the world, and of the necessity to *actively* fight such evil. In modern times, Hitler picked a specific day and year to begin his extermination program against the Jews. That day was the ninth day of the Hebrew month Ab, the day that all the major tragedies occurred that beset the Jews throughout their history: the destruction of the first and second temples; the beginning of the Spanish Inquisition, amongst others.

One of our major tasks in life is to make constant corrections and atonements for our errors, which are a constant assaults against truth. Acting in truth creates disturbing feelings to melt away. We all know the truth. It is not possible to live on earth in a functional way relating in a socially adaptive or an anti-socially maladaptive way without knowing truth. We are all born with the capacity to know it and to act on it, but we give in early in life to all the social pressures exerted on us and conform to the mass conscious tendency to suppress it and support the lies heaped on us under the threat of physical harm and death. At the basis of living outside of truth lies feelings of guilt for not behaving the way we are meant to. Ideally, we need not feel guilty about anything we do when we recognize the necessity to face and take responsibility for what we do and act accordingly to make corrections. Taking such action removes guilt feelings.

When you become aware of suffering, *always* ask yourself what you may be feeling guilty about. Feelings of guilt are the emotional component at the core of all suffering. In addition, we are always combatting within ourselves the mental factors of doubt, expectation, and denial, which are the seed sources of *all* our problems. Indeed, these four factors are involved in, and are at the root of all human suffering on earth. In my book *Healing Into Immortality,* I outlined the ways we have for overcoming doubt, expectation, denial. But for now I want to give attention to guilt feelings.

Guilt feelings are really an artifact of our life in that they are unnecessary and actually unwarranted. That guilt feelings are ubiquitous in a large segment of people does not make them valid. Real as they are when we feel them, and as natural as they may be to experience them, nonetheless they are not normal to maintain over any extended period of time. That they linger in consciousness means that we haven't dealt directly with the issue to which they refer.

In addition, feelings of guilt keep us tied to the past and away from the present moment. Chronic feelings of guilt give rise also to a state of depression, again keeping us riveted to the past. Being tied to the past is to murder ourselves, to commit partial suicide, to live in the grasp of evil. Feeling guilty is tantamount to being in a state of mental paralysis.

If you feel guilty you may find that confessing whatever it is plaguing you can be rather relieving. The confession I have in mind is that described by Philo three centuries before part of his technique became a cornerstone of the teachings of the Catholic Church. His technique was two-pronged: confession of the heart and confession of the lips. The first is to confess your error to yourself and to ask your higher self or ask God for forgiveness. Then confess your error to the one you've wronged and ask for forgiveness if the circumstances permit and are relevant.

The great gift bestowed on us through the story of Queen Esther is this great moral lesson of giving credit to our sources. To do the opposite is to steal something from someone, claim it as your own, and behave as though that person does not exist. All this is done so as to elevate your own position, reap the rewards thereby all at the expense of the original author who characteristically is not compensated and suffers emotionally more than anyone can imagine.

134 CLIMBING JACOB'S LADDER

Telling the truth is not a common commodity we encounter on earth. So much of human history has been marked by the enmity people have shown to one another, being prompted to do so by the lies fed them by their rulers. Thus, Esther's story is one of truth; how truth prevailed over lying and calumny. Hence, she fulfilled the eighth and ninth commandments.

It is of interest to note that wherever there has been a Jewish presence in the world, it has called forth an impulse from a group or nation to exterminate it. So, this story bears special attention for what it has to tell us about how and what the intervention was that permitted those yoked to God to live. We can see from the story something about the roots of anti-Semitism, which has to exist in the world unless and until the monotheistic people carry out the covenant struck with God to become a "kingdom of priests" and "a holy nation" (Exodus 19:6). It seems that a foundational point at the heart of this contract, and focused on directly in Esther, is the emphasis on truth. Another defining characteristic of truth is its connection with the present, the now moment, the what IS of our immediate experience. Placing our attention on the future or the past brings us into two illusory realms, meaning that neither of them exist: the former hasn't happened yet, and the latter is finished, over and done with. Neither of them have any inherent connection with the present moment. Within this moment is contained the essential core pattern of our life as it has unfolded from birth . As well, this moment also gives birth to the future. Neither the past nor future moment give birth to our present moment. The present is not predicated on the past or future. Rather, it is quite the other way around. The moment gives meaning to what has transpired, and will dictate what is to transpire.

For instance, when we are worried or fearful, the *context* of these real feelings is always about the future. Some people may experience an urgency to cheat, steal, lie, even commit murder because of what they are afraid they may be without, won't have, or be deprived of if they don't act to fortify and preserve themselves against some perceived danger to their survival. When we seethe about the past, about the slights or insults we may have received, we begin to feel angry, leading to vengeful feelings eventuating in initiating some malicious or retributive act against someone.

Thinking into the future or past invariably leads us into trouble. Anywhere God isn't in our thoughts we are inclining toward, or are facing evil. God's domain, as far as we are concerned, is the present moment. Brushing away all thoughts not centered in the present helps to keep us in the present. Being in the present gives us peace, happiness, unburdening, and lightness.

It is said in the Western tradition that we are to carry our burdens lightly and to wear our yoke easily. To be burdened is to suffer. To suffer is to bear; and it is the nature of life to have to suffer the consequences of our actions and thoughts that have not been in truth. Understanding this fact is very beneficial I have found in my own experience, both personally and in my clinical practice. It is a key to healing to know that which pains us is giving us the opportunity to make a correction in our lives that puts us on the road of truth and freedom. In effect, we welcome pain, but we are not to dwell in the pain.

As soon as we recognize that pain is a reflection of our behavior — internally and externally — then we take immediate steps to rectify the error(s). To remain indwelling in pain depletes us of our vital resources and makes us age, decay, and die. It serves no life-affirming purpose to linger in pain, and as we become weakened from prolonged pain, we fall prey to outside influences as our will diminishes.[7]

To appreciate the falsity of future thinking, I would recommend that you take one day and make note of how many anticipations, expectations, plans, promises, all having to do with the future, do or don't come to fruition in that given day. If you like, expand this inquiry to as many days as you like and don't forget to make note of how much turns out and doesn't turn out.

* * *

So, the story of Esther is about God's presence on earth, as it resides in the depths of consciousness of a handful of people devoted to Monotheism here which can never be extinguished. Without the existence of these special souls, this planet might have already met an ominous fate. Queen Esther is working for the force of life that resides in all of us that is seeking to triumph over the force of death that waits for us when the light of life and the life of light stops burning in us.

DANIEL: PROPHET OF DISCIPLINE AND DESTINY

Daniel was a prophet living in exile in Babylon (ancient Iraq) under the reign of King Nebuchadnezzar II and his son Belshazzar. He was recognized for his prophetic prowess and his visions of what is coming for us in *this age* of the end of days. He was employed by Nebuchadnezzar to read dreams, which had the effect of helping to save the kingdom (much like Daniel's predecessor Joseph in Egypt with Pharaoh). Nebuchadnezzar was grateful for Daniel's efforts and recognized the greatness of Daniel's monotheistic God over all other gods, including his own. However, this feeling cannot be sustained, and under the influence of his own ministers, who want to destroy the Jews, is turned against Daniel in spite of his good will. On that occasion, Daniel's companions — Shadrach, Meshach, Abednego — are ordered to enter a fiery furnace to "prove" that Daniel's God is great. The three are not scathed at all and emerge unchanged even though the heat is turned up as high as possible. (The modern analogy to Hitler's use of the fiery furnace is inescapable.)

There is another well-known incident associated with this giant amongst prophets. It concerns Belshazzar, son of Nebuchadnezzar. After the latter destroyed the Temple in 586 BCE and sacked it, Belshazzar used the stolen silver goblets to serve wine to his guests at a banquet. Suddenly, a giant finger appeared and wrote an indecipherable message on the wall — "Mene, Mene, Tekel, Upharsin" — for which only Daniel could decipher. The most well-known story of Daniel is his being cast into a den of lions to test whether his God could save him from certain death. Daniel emerges unharmed, the lions having been subdued, his God triumphant.

In the midst of all the sumptuous wealth of Babylonia, Daniel is not impressed nor influenced. Daniel is the model of how to live a life of spirit amongst a world much like ours, committed to material life and life of the senses. Throughout the story, Daniel forgoes all temptations of material wealth to stay true to his path of serving God. In doing so he is able to take the forces of instinctual life represented by the lions, those forces of territoriality and acquisition represented by lions, pushing us to acquire more than we can possibly use. He has effectively taken a vow of poverty and with that, he gained the riches of the life of spirit, being filled with the gift of prophecy, the quality of clear-sightedness indicated by his ability to see and read the handwriting on the wall.

Additionally, Daniel never accepts the practices of idolatry in which the Babylonians revel. In fact, he warns King Nebuchadnezzar and later King Belshazzar of the dangerous consequences of idolatry, from which they both suffered. The lesson of history about worshipping idols is made eminently clear in his story. The analogy to our modern life: We are worshippers of gold, silver, brass, and iron in all their manifold forms, hypnotized as we are by the shiny objects dangled in front of our eyes and the hypnotic suggestions blared into our ears endlessly.

He does not follow the conventions, nor the conventional mores and faces dire punishment for his dedication to God. He is never open to suggestion and is certainly a man of authority — self-authority.

One of Daniel's outstanding characteristics was his ability to stand up to authority, to the seemingly strong and powerful. His is a case of the weak versus the strong. The paradox here is that of the reversing process played out in the story. In truth, Daniel appears to be the weak one, while Kings Nebuchadnezzar and Belshazzar are the mighty ones, but actually the opposite is the case. Daniel is supported by God and demonstrates his might before these kings, who represent a godless people steeped in material life, which had become the god of Babylonia. His story is very much a version of David's battle with Goliath.

Daniel is a being who displayed that courage to forgo the outer life for the inner life. He also was brave, the outward show of courage that he displayed toward tyranny. His behavior demonstrated the truth of an axiom of spiritual practice: *never* appease an irrational force. Never appease a Nazi, either, in your personal life, or in the life of the collective. Appeasement, in this case, is *always* the action of the false self in us that attaches itself to the manmade world, anticipating that this world can provide us with what we think we need to become happy and satisfied in life.

Daniel has many important things to say about preparing ourselves for the life of Spirit. For example, changing one's diet. He did not eat the food of the Babylonians, instead accepting to eat a diet that was cleansing and detoxifying. Not eating the food of the country also means not to take on the value system of the herd. In this regard, applying the story to modern life we can easily see how America is modern Babylonia, whose value system is squarely centered on greed flying in the face of the Tenth Commandment of not coveting. We are easily one of the most covetous nations on earth, with no end in sight.

Indeed, within this rudderless nation there is a spiritual ferment and an awakening consciousness to the value of Spirit. To make this turn meaningfully and not self-deceptively, we must follow the Daniel mode and take his prescription for spiritual development: take the vow of poverty, absent ourselves from the predominant value system, have faith in the certainty of God, and do not be open to suggestion.

Much of what he saw could be analogized to modern times, presaging the development of modern industrial life, the advent of Hitler, and the dawning of the times in which we now live known as the Messianic Age. He describes a day of judgment and an end of days, meaning a shift in consciousness transcending the murderous, violent consciousness that has characterized the twentieth century.

As I said, Daniel is the prophet for the end of days, the time of the Messiah, the dawning of the consciousness of love. He is showing the way we need to prepare for this momentous time, which we are, in fact, in right now. He heralds the time when we arise out of the ashes, like the mythical Phoenix who died by fire and arose anew out of its own ashes. As a contemporary analogy, out of the ashes of the Holocaust arose the state of Israel, born again — resurrected as it were like the Phoenix — to be given another chance to carry out the covenant to possibly become a kingdom of priests.

I mentioned earlier that Daniel deciphered the handwriting on the wall — the words "mene, mene, tekel, upharsin." In Daniel 5:26-28 the reading is given : "MENE, God hath numbered thy kingdom, and brought it to and end. TEKEL, thou art weighed in the balances, and are found wanting. PERES, thy Kingdom is divided, and given to the Medes and Persians." That night Belshazzar was murdered. Daniel was made one of three to rule in the kingdom for his reading. Later on, when Darius took over the kingdom he sought to set Daniel as the next in command under him. It was this announcement that stirred Darius's other ministers to speak slanderously against him and have Darius sign the decree to have Daniel cast into the lion's den.

It is from this reading that comes the common phrase "the handwriting on the wall." To read the handwriting is to read the signs for yourself or possibly for someone else. Once the sign is read, immediate action is required. The message is clear, given by the universe, and enjoins us to do whatever is required regardless of what we may have to give up or sacrifice. These universal messages are blessings to give us direction to take, which may save us or rectify a circumstance that is becoming destructive. In Belshazzar's case, Daniel was asked only to read the message. He was not asked what to do about the message. Had Belshazzar done so, perhaps he would have acted to save his life. However, it was highly unlikely because the indictment and judgment were already rendered from on high, and his "fate" was sealed.

Learning to read the signs is a language we all need to embrace. All the knowledge we ever need for ourselves in conducting our lives is reflected in the signs. Images are a sign language as well as a symbol one. Sign means something concrete pointing to something else that is concrete. For instance, when going to a public bathroom, the sign/image of a woman or man on the door points to the respective bathroom. Symbol refers to an image pointing to something invisible — a quality or invisible function having no immediate concrete reference point. For example, the image of a bear is a symbol of resurrection; a dove a symbol of peace; a beaver a symbol of industriousness. These symbols may point to something sacred, such as does the Star of David, or point to some possibility available to human existence, like the three mentioned above. Both sign or symbol are acknowledging and drawing our attention to a type of thinking underlying spiritual awakening — at least for Western practitioners. This thinking is termed "analogy," to see the correspondences between things; to see the mirror reflection of one thing to another. This latter point has significance for us because the reflection can be between the visible and invisible domains.

As you may know, analogy means two things being related to each other by having similarities in common, although they are not exactly alike. One case that exemplifies this understanding is when we put our hand up to a mirror. What is reflected back is a hand that is quite similar to that one but is not exactly alike. For, when putting up the left hand, for example, what is reflected is the right hand in the mirror. Another type of example is that found in Genesis 1:26 about our being made in God's image and likeness. That phrase refers, in one way, to the fact of analogy. We are created as mirror reflections of God. We are actually reflections of the reflection of God, as my teacher Colette pointed out to me. We are analogies of God — the mirror image of Him.

For example, the lungs are the visible reflection of freedom, a non-visible quality. So, qualities and quantities mirror each other. Understanding this mirroring can help us understand the meaning of illness on a practical level. When a problem occurs in a certain part of the body, we seek to find its meaning on another level: gall bladder, for example, corresponds to envy or jealousy on the emotional level. Knowledge of this sort is of inestimable value in aiding our healing process.

Pertinent to Daniel, as I discussed in "Joseph," is the use of analogy in dream reading. You will find it most helpful, when you dream, to ask yourself the question: "What is the analogy of my waking life to this dream experience?" When you ask the question in this way, you will generally get an immediate answer that deepens the meaning of your life experience, and which may provide an answer to a life situation with which you may be currently struggling. Using the analogy method is one of the immediate ways that Daniel — and Joseph — gleaned the meanings of the enigmatic dreams posed to them. In the events in the Bible, the dreamer was not asked for their understanding of the dream analogy as we would do working with dreams, as the dreamer is the final arbiter. Instead, those sages were given full license to educe the meaning only after the dreamer had been unable to glean a meaning.

Learning to read the signs is to learn to look at what is, let it speak to/through you as an intuitive flash, and act on it. Seeing the "is" of something is to capture the moment. There is *no need* to add any commentary or opinion to it. To do so it so lose the full impact — of here, now, the moment — the realm of truth and freedom. Only what is has value, *no matter* what that experience may be. You don't have to know what the value may be. Just know it has value and don't run away to "it shouldn't be like this, it ought to be . . ." Stay with the "isness" of the perception and an answer will come to you. The first voice — of God — will speak to you, and tell you the truth. In this way we can begin to fulfill our Daniel nature.

CHAPTER FIVE

EXPERIENTIAL IMAGERY:
LIVING THE BIBLE IN IMAGINATION

What promotes our ascent of the ladder of self-mastery is mental imagery. It is a primary tool of spiritual practice in the monotheistic direction of inner vision. By tapping into our inner repository of stored wisdom, and also using this process of mind to make contact with beings on other levels of reality, or planes of existence, we can create new realities and experiences in everyday existence and find a transcendent connection with God. With imagination we can transform our relationship to the world around us in a constructive, healing way, and turn to Spirit to find a meaningful path to marrying God.

Imagery gives us direct access to universal experience transcending linear time and three-dimensional space. With respect to the Bible stories, living the imagery experience gives us direct knowledge of the quality to which we are directed by each story; we experience the pitfalls and possibilities awaiting us and affecting the outcomes of our lives.

It is understood in the Western tradition that we are born with free will and at the same time we are participating in a grand cosmic plan that is already blueprinted and moves inexorably toward its fulfillment. Each of us lives out our part of the plan. When we have gone astray from our inherent divinity, the universe reveals to us what we are doing and have done. The universe provides us with all the knowledge we need about ourselves.

The knowledge is revealed to us in the language of image. Every event we encounter is always experienced imaginally. They can happen as an internal event as in inner imagery experience, daydreams, hallucinations, night dreams. Or, we can live direct experience of the senses in the external waking world. Our everyday life is as imaginal as any inner event, and needs to be read initially as a reflection of some quality or characteristic of ourselves. All imagery experience, no matter where we encounter it, has *always* to be read initially as relating to something referable to some aspect of the "I." This is part of what I mean by the comment that "everything" is within Divine Providence and has a meaning!

The image is a revelatory experience, and by definition has a meaning in the constant interaction going on between God and us. For every human being a message is being sent, uniquely for each one of us, to give us guidance and direction for our lives. For example, if Jonah has disobeyed God, a message is sent in the form of a great storm, which he deciphers and subsequently takes the appropriate action. Whatever it is necessary for us to know about our lives, a message will be delivered accordingly, either through an inner image experience, such as Pharaoh's dream, or through some external event presenting itself, like the "handwriting on the wall," itself having now become a phrase about reading messages.

The cosmos unfolds itself to us and how we fit into the plan, i.e., to find our individual way to God, each in our unique way. Where free will comes in is that we are free to choose what to do with the knowledge. We can heed the call being shown us, or we can go in whatever direction we decide. No matter what we do, the universe will return to us exactly what we need. We are receiving teaching and guidance all the time from the universe. Actually, our own lived experience becomes our teacher and learning tool. Learning to read the messages does away with the need for external teachers, and eliminates then another possibility for getting caught in the tug of idolatry by coming to worship an outer authority.

Learning to read the images is at the heart of the intuitive process. It brings us back to the footsteps of God as the restorative process that corrects the error made in Eden. That error involved our wanting to replace knowledge through revelation, by knowledge through experimentation. The former is knowledge of/in the present instant and is a direct link between ourselves and God. The image is the language of the instant that gives us knowledge. We are able to translate that inner knowledge directly into outer action. We act immediately as conduits between God and the world. We don't question that knowledge but instead plunge from perception directly to action. This is the practice of faith.

All of the exercises presented here are of my own creation except for those of Abraham, Moses, and one each of Daniel and Jonah, which were created by Colette; one on David created by Dr. Celia Blumenthal; and one of Adam and Eve created by my student Frances Greenfield. I have placed an asterisk next to these exercises to identify them.

Before embarking on the exercises, let me give you some instruction about doing imagery work.

IMAGERY EXERCISES — GENERAL INSTRUCTIONS

Mental imagery succeeds in direct proportion to how successfully you can turn your senses away from the outside world and toward your inner realm. Once you are turned inward, you can evoke a mental image that can stimulate your physical body. The image will come to you on its own, as long as you direct your will and attention inward.

You may find that exercises that I have designed for a specific use apply to other difficulties with which you are coping. This is perfectly acceptable, since mental imagery exercises have a "crossover" effect and can be used for different purposes.

Body Posture

The most effective body position for imaging is what I call the Pharaoh's Posture. Sit upright in a straight-backed chair that has armrests, your back straight, your arms resting comfortably on the armrests, and your hands open, palms down. Your feet should be flat on the floor. Neither your hands nor your feet should be crossed during the imagery work; nor should they come into contact with any other part of your body. This arrangement is part of keeping your sensory awareness focused away from external stimuli.

Throughout the ages, the Pharaoh's Posture was assumed by royalty who sought their inner guides before making a decision. It is a posture expressing the search for inner guidance.

A straight-backed chair is best because a straight spine permits a sense of awareness to infuse our attention. Lying down, in either a horizontal or a reclining position, is associated with sleeping and reduces the heightened awareness required for mental imagery.

Sitting with your back straight also enhances your breathing; your lungs need this vertical posture in order to expand fully. Awareness of breath, as all ancient physicians and healers knew, promotes greater alertness and attentiveness to mental processes. We become more attuned to our inner life as we become more conscious of our breathing.

While the Pharaoh's Posture is ideally suited to imagery work, sometimes imagery must be done without it — for example, when you are experiencing anxiety. In these situations, you may do the imagery work standing up, wherever you may be.

Breathing

Breathing plays an essential role in all inner-directed experience. Those who meditate become relaxed and quiet by counting their breaths. The Chinese equate breath with the mind itself. Yoga exercise, natural childbirth, martial arts, running, or any other sport involving concentrated intention, all focus on breath.

Most of us are not generally aware of our breathing. Nor are we usually comfortable directing ourselves to our inner life. We are an active people with urges to conquer the outside world and master nature. But the inner life holds the cure to our physical and emotional imbalances and the promise of harmony between body, mind, and eventually Spirit. Breathing allows the inward turning to occur; it is the link that enables us to discover our personal imagery.

To enhance the presence of images, give yourself the intention of becoming quiet and relaxed. Breathe rhythmically, *in through the nose and out through the mouth*. The exhalations through the mouth should be longer and slower than the inhalations, which are normal and easy — neither labored nor exaggerated. Breathing out longer than breathing in stimulates the vagus nerve, the major quieting nerve in the body. Originating at the base of the brain, in the medulla, this nerve extends down through the neck and sends branches to the lungs, heart, and intestinal tract.

Influenced by enhanced exhalation, the vagus plays a role in lowering blood pressure, slowing the pulse, heart rate, and muscular contractions of the intestinal tract, and reducing the respiratory rate. When these functions are quiet, your attention is more fully available for imagery work.

I stress exhalation over inhalation because breathing to quiet the body begins with an *outbreath,* not an *inbreath.* The more usual in-out breathing stimulates us by exciting our sympathetic or excitatory nervous system and the adrenal medulla, which secretes adrenaline. Out-in breathing on the other hand, stimulates the parasympathetic nervous system and the vagus nerve, which help the body quiet down.

When you are comfortable with your breathing and feel ready to begin your imagery work, *breathe out three times*. This may sound odd, but it is quite simple. You breathe out, then in; out, then in; then out again — for a total of three out-breaths and two inbreaths. After this you begin your imagery exercise, breathing regularly.

During your imagery work, your attention will be focused on the images, and your breathing will take care of itself. When the imagery event is ended, you take one out-breath before opening your eyes.

It will take you only a few seconds to establish this reverse breathing pattern. Exhaling first and inhaling second will become second nature once you have learned to image. Finally, in the instructions for the exercises, BO = breathe out; 1X, 2X, 3X = one times, two times, three times.

Length of Exercises

Do each exercise quickly! The value of imagery lies in the light shock that it gives to your system, which promotes healing. You only need a spark. It only takes the flame of one small match to set off all the fireworks. Healing is prompted by this sudden jolt. Healing through imagery is like the home-opathic process in that a minute amount of substance stimulates the body's healing response. The rule of thumb for imagery work is that *less is more*. The shorter the imagery, the more powerful its power.

Imagery has to stimulate inner movement. We experience this vital inner movement as sensation or emotion. While sensations are physical, emotions are inner mental movements analogous to physical movements, themselves acts of will. When movements occur inside, they are life.

Imagery is the form that that movement takes. If you experience a stimulus or shock, coming from either an external or internal source, you respond. Therefore, making your imagery move you inside will mean that it is potent.

It does not have to take long to experience a sensation. The sensations vary from person to person and problem to problem, but they often include twitching, pulsation, heat, itching, pain, tingling, a buzz, and the like. Once you have felt the sensation, the imagery has done its work. If you don't feel a sensation after a relatively short period of time, do not strive for it by repeating that particular image. Instead, try another one.

Many think that expending more effort brings more results, but with imagery the opposite is true. Most exercises in this book take up to or about one minute to do. Many people feel that this is less time than they could or should be spending, particularly for serious ailments. Their anxiety creates the idea that they must "spare no effort." But strenuous application of effort is simply not necessary in imagery work. Once you have done an initial imagery experience, you need only little reminders to stimulate your body's recollection of healing activity. You need to practice imagery, but it should not become an obsession. One trigger is all you need to promote physiological repair mechanisms. The Russian psychologist Ivan Pavlov conditioned dogs to salivate at the sound of a bell. In imagery work, we condition ourselves to stimulate healing with a mental picture. Like Pavlov's bell, the image is the stimulus, and like the dog's salivation, the healing process is the response.

Before beginning each imagery exercise *always* give yourself the name of the exercise, the intention, and how long it is taking; *all* said to yourself *in the present tense*. For example: "I am doing the freedom exercises to find spiritual freedom and it is taking me five seconds each." Your biological clock will have you open your eyes at the proper time.

* * *

FREEDOM

INTENTION: To find spiritual freedom

FREQUENCY: Each morning, first thing, up to 30 seconds for numbers 1 and 2. For number 3, do any combination or all any time you remember for up to 5 seconds each except for the Dot exercise, which is to take an instant.

1. Close your eyes. BO 3X. Live and know why freedom cannot be connected directly to our physical relationship to life. Breathe out and open your eyes.

2. Close your eyes. BO 3X. See, feel, and sense how without being in a physical body freedom cannot happen. Breathe out and open your eyes.

3. Close your eyes. BO 1X. Experience yourself as a dot in the center of a circle. BO 1X. See, sense and live the present moment as no time. BO 3X. Sense and feel how the imagery process allows us to live the presence of the present. Breathe out and open your eyes. (For this number 3 group, if done in combination, eyes remain closed.)

* * *

EDEN

INTENTION: To experience Eden.

FREQUENCY: Once a year at the same time and date for 30 seconds.

1. Close your eyes. BO 1X. See, sense, feel, and live yourself in the garden of your inner reality. Become immersed in the full-

ness of God's truth. Hear the universe echoing *Hallelujah!* Remember this image as you breathe out and open your eyes. See the image on the wall opposite you and let it fade away.

* * *

ADAM AND EVE

INTENTION: To know yourself as Adam and Eve.

FREQUENCY: Once a year at the same time and date for 30 seconds each.

1.* Close your eyes. BO 3X. See, sense, and feel how God is blowing into you the breath of life. BO 1X. Know, sense, and see how this breath is the spark that ignites your life force. BO 1X. Feel and see this breath spreading throughout every part of your body, through each organ and cell, filling you with blue-golden light. Know and live how this sparkling health is giving you new life, and is infusing you with will, joyfulness, and the power to heal. Breathe out and open your eyes.

2. Close your eyes. BO 3X. Become Eve being born from the rib of Adam. Know the meaning of the rib as the support of the chest, the place of courage, bravery, and fearlessness. Live this intimacy with Adam. BO 3X. As Adam, be aware of how being in unity *has* to give rise to the *necessity* for two in preparation for living in the world of the serpent. Be accepting of this reality without sadness. Breathe out and open your eyes.

3. Close your eyes. BO 2X. See, feel, and sense the power of the serpent's words to you promising you to become God. BO 3X. Know why, even though God sends the serpent to test

Adam and Eve, he still has to be punished by God. Breathe out and open your eyes.

4. Close your eyes. BO 3X. See yourself as Eve leading Adam into life. BO 1X. Be Adam accepting to follow Eve. Know how only by men accepting the wisdom of women can love come to replace discord. Breathe out and open your eyes.

* * *

CAIN AND ABEL

INTENTION: To know your Cain and Abel nature.

FREQUENCY: Once a year at the same time and date for 30 seconds.

1. Close your eyes. BO 3X. Be Cain. BO 1X. Be Abel. Whom do you experience more strongly? Don't judge either. Breathe out and open your eyes.

2. Close your eyes. BO 3X. Know how we let the weak rule the strong in our everyday life. BO 1X. Refuse to be sacrificed in this way. Breathe out and open your eyes.

3. Close your eyes. BO 3X. As Abel, offer your first fruits to God. Know how you become closer to Him by this offering. Breathe out and open your eyes.

4. Close your eyes. BO 2X. Be Cain wandering in the world with the mark on your forehead. Know what it is to wander in this way and why vengeance cannot be taken against you. Breathe out and open your eyes.

5. Close your eyes. BO 2X. See, feel, and live as Cain becoming the richest person in the world, even though you have

committed an iniquity. Know now why the "triumph" of materialism has brought decay to our life individually and socially. Breathe out and open your eyes.

6. Close your eyes. BO 3X. Be your brother's keeper. What do you feel? BO 3X. Feel and know how this quality brings peace and harmony to life. Breathe out and open your eyes.

* * *

ABRAHAM*

INTENTION: To become faithful.

FREQUENCY: Once a year at the same time and date for 30 seconds.

1. Close your eyes and BO 3X. Hear as Abraham the command "Go to yourself" *(lech lecha* in Hebrew). Feel awakened, renewed, renovated, and resurrected. Breathe out and open your eyes.

2. Close your eyes and BO 3X. Be as Abraham, the one of unsurpassed challenges and feeling the necessity to do them. Breathe out and open your eyes.

3. Close your eyes and BO 3X. Live as Abraham, the breaker of the idols. Breathe out and open your eyes.

4. Close your eyes and BO 3X. Feel and know in yourself the total change and newness when breaking with the commonly accepted way of life. Breathe out and open your eyes.

5. Close your eyes and BO 3X. Know and sense all that as potential is now reality and is already present in you, always with you. Breathe out and open your eyes.

6. Close your eyes and BO 1X. See and choose your own way. Have a blueprint of it and go ahead. Breathe out and open your eyes.

* * *

LOT AND LOT'S WIFE

INTENTION: To experience righteousness and expel regret.

FREQUENCY: Once a year at the same time and date for 30 seconds.

1. Close your eyes and BO 3X. See, sense, and feel yourself as Lot: righteous, generous, and understanding. Breathe out and open your eyes.

2. Close your eyes and BO 3X. See and know the errors created by the acts of men and women in Sodom and Gomorrah. BO 1X. Now, become aware of the errors you make in everyday life to create your own Sodom and Gomorrah when we are not righteous, generous, and understanding. Breathe out and open your eyes.

3. Close your eyes and BO 3X. Sense and feel the reluctance to leave people you love when it is necessary for you to take on a new way of life. Sense a moment of sadness at having no choice but to leave them. BO 1X. Rejoice at the new choice you have made to turn to Spirit for your sake and theirs. Breathe out and open your eyes.

4. Close your eyes and BO 3X. Become Lot's wife feeling regret at having to give up what is familiar. Sense this attachment to the past, even though that past was, or may have been, painful. Sense and experience the tears welling up at seeing the loss associated with the past. BO 1X. As the tears

fall, see yourself becoming a pillar of salt, yourself hardening from the salt of the tears of regret about the past. Know how we sclerose when we attach ourselves to the pain of the past and the regrets connected with it. Breathe out 2X — Realize how all of these tears have made you live disconnected to the moment of now, where lie all of our possibilities. BO 1X. With a large hose of warm, spiraling blue water, wash away all the salt from your body, inside and out. Feel yourself becoming renewed and revived with this newly found wisdom and find yourself turning to a new future, to see what is there for you in this new instant. Breathe out and open your eyes.

* * *

JACOB

INTENTION: To know self-transformation.

FREQUENCY: Once a year at the same time and date for 30 seconds.

1. Close your eyes and BO 3X. Be Jacob, the youth of contemplation. BO 1X. Be Esau, the youth of cunning and hunting. BO 1X. Choose whom you wish to become. Don't judge your choice. Breathe out and open your eyes.

2. Close your eyes. BO 3X. Go to Isaac as Jacob impersonating Esau. What do you feel? Hear what Isaac tells to you, and know your life's mission. Breathe out and open your eyes.

3. Close your eyes and BO 3X. Work for fourteen years to fulfill your quest for what or whom you love. How do you feel? Know the true value of work. Breathe out and open your eyes.

4. Close your eyes. BO 2X. Live and know the deception against Esau. BO 2X. Live and know the deception of Leah against Jacob. BO 2X. Live and know the deception of Jacob's sons disclosing Joseph's "death" to Jacob. BO 3X. Live, know, and feel, without judgment, the value and vice of deception . Breathe out and open your eyes.

5. Close your eyes. BO 3X. Experience the ascending and descending of the angels on the ladder. Feel and sense the transformation coming with the presence of the ladder. BO 1X. Let the angels escort you along the ladder. Be thankful for their presence. Breathe out and open your eyes.

6. Close your eyes. BO 3X. Be as Jacob wrestling with the angel. Experience this struggle with God's messenger. Be grateful for the injury you sustain reminding you of your spiritual transformation. BO 1X. Hear your name being changed, and the sound this new name makes; know that your transformation is now in place. Breathe out and open your eyes.

* * *

JOSEPH

INTENTION: To become awakened.

FREQUENCY: Once a year at the same time and date for 30 seconds.

1. Close your eyes. BO 3X. Be as Joseph wearing your dream coat of many colors telling your brothers the dream of the eleven sheaves of wheat. What do you experience, i.e., sense and feel? BO 1X. Now, be any of the brothers hearing the dream. What do you sense and feel? Breathe out and open your eyes.

2. Close your eyes. BO 3X. See, sense, feel, and live yourself thrown in the pit. Understand why this was done to you. Let it now become a teaching for you. Breathe out and open your eyes.

3. Close your eyes. BO 3X. With this new understanding, accept your new life away from everything that has been familiar to you. BO 1X. Know what it is to be a "stranger in a strange land." Breathe out and open your eyes.

4. Close your eyes. BO 3X. Find yourself transforming into the master statesman, having used your gifts for the good of all. Know how using your gifts in this way has made possible this transformation. Breathe out and open your eyes.

5. Close your eyes. BO 3X. You are Joseph receiving your brothers who have come to ask for help. BO 3X. Sense and feel yourself without anger or vengeance. How do you experience this breaking of a reflexive habit pattern? Breathe out and open your eyes.

6. Close your eyes. BO 3X. Feel, as Joseph, the new life, light, and wisdom that your exile has brought you. BO 1X. Be reconciled with your old family in a new way. Breathe out and open your eyes.

* * *

MOSES*

INTENTION: To become a leader.

FREQUENCY: Once a year at the same time and date for 30 seconds.

1. Close your eyes. BO 3X. See and feel yourself as Moses going up the mountainside with a flock of sheep. You come to the top and the sheep are grazing. *Suddenly* you feel intense heat all around enveloping you. Fire breaks out and the burning bush appears in front of you, cutting you off from the flock. What happens? Breathe out and open your eyes.

2. Close your eyes and BO 3X. You are Moses, the Prince of Egypt. You are helping the Jews to construct the pyramid. What happens? Breathe out and open your eyes.

3. Close your eyes. BO 3X. You are Moses leading the people into the desert. Many of them are being bitten and poisoned by snakes. How do you feel and what do you do? Breathe out and open your eyes.

4. Close your eyes. BO 3X. You are Moses climbing Mount Sinai. Feel yourself leaving the mass of people below. Finally, reaching the top you sit and fast, asking God whatever question you wish answered. Then, with the tablets, descend the mountain, and describe what happens. Breathe out and open your eyes.

5. Close your eyes. BO 3X. You are Moses in the desert with the people. There is no water and the people are desperate for water. Experience the feelings of the people and the seventy elders. What do you feel and what do you do? Breathe out and open your eyes.

6. Close your eyes. BO 3X. The red heifer is in the desert. The specialists are showing the people the meaning of this cow. What is happening? Be among the people. Be the specialists and know the meaning of this cow. Breathe out and open your eyes.

* * *

SAMSON

INTENTION: To feel your strength and to become chaste.

FREQUENCY: Once a year at the same time and date for 30 seconds.

1. Close your eyes. BO 3X. See, sense, feel, live, and know the strength of Samson being born with a full head of thick, curly hair. Breathe out and open your eyes.

2. Close your eyes. BO 3X. Be as Samson taming the lion of your instinctual urges. Do so with your bare hands. Have no qualms about breaking the jaw of the beast. BO 1X. See the bees in the body of the lion making honey. Know that the reward for taming your instincts becomes the sweetness of life. Breathe out and open your eyes.

3. Close your eyes. BO 3X. See, sense, feel, and know that we may still be seduced and tempted by the temporary pleasures of this world, as Samson was by the Philistines. Breathe out and open your eyes.

4. Close your eyes. BO 1X. Feel and know yourself tricking and in turn being tricked by the forces of the will to power in the form of Delilah. Know how she wins this game when we are not vigilant. BO 2X. Know that when we are not vigilant

we lose sight of our purpose in life, and as Samson, can be made blind. Breathe out and open your eyes.

5. Close your eyes. BO 3X. See, sense, and feel yourself as Samson redeeming the error of intoxication by conquering the enslavers in their temples. BO 1X. Feel yourself becoming closer to God. Breathe out and open your eyes.

6. Close your eyes. BO 3X. See yourself with your angel of the Lord ascending up the fiery flame to God. Keep those feelings and what you experience for yourself. Breathe out and open your eyes.

* * *

DAVID

INTENTION: To become fearless and king/queen of yourself.

FREQUENCY: Once a year at the same time and date for 30 seconds.

1. Close your eyes. BO 3X. See, feel, and know how, as David, you are able to fearlessly face the giant Goliath. BO 1X. Recognize how the smallest of substances can conquer what seems to be the most overwhelming. Breathe out and open your eyes.

2. Close your eyes. BO 3X. See yourself as David tending to King Saul, the one who wants to kill you. Be unafraid as you minister to him and administer your healing refrains. What do you feel? What happens? Know the difference between acceptance and forgiveness. Breathe out and open your eyes.

3.* Close your eyes. BO 3X. Be as David embodying the four male archetypes: warrior, wise man, father (king), lover. BO

3X. Use your strongest archetype to support the weakest. What do you know and feel in this connection? Breathe out and open your eyes.

4. Close your eyes. BO 3X. Experience the unconditional love of Jonathan for David, then David for Jonathan. Know and understand why unconditional love transcends all other human experience. Breathe out and open your eyes.

5. Close your eyes. BO 3X. Be Jonathan, giving up his throne for David. BO 3X. See and know how without sacrifice — giving without having to get — unconditional love is impossible. Breathe out and open your eyes.

6. Close your eyes. BO 3X. See yourself writing a psalm of praise, recording all that you have learned from the preceding exercises. Breathe out and open your eyes and physically write this paean.

* * *

JONAH

INTENTION: To become obedient.

FREQUENCY: Once a year at the same time and date for 30 seconds.

1. Close your eyes. BO 3X. Hear, as Jonah, an inner voice speaking to you, telling you to do what you don't habitually like to do. Know why you are reluctant to obey. Breathe out and open your eyes.

2. Close your eyes. BO 3X. See and feel yourself, as Jonah, running away in rebellion to what you know is your responsibility. BO 1X. Live how painful it is to have

responsibility and to avoid responsibility. Breathe out and open your eyes.

3. Close your eyes. BO 3X. See, sense, and feel yourself being caught by the forces of nature and feeling threatened. You awaken to your error by this shock. Ask the crew of the boat, whose lives your action has imperiled, to throw you overboard. BO 3X. Know and live the great merit you receive by sacrificing yourself for the sake of the greater community. Breathe out and open your eyes.

4. Close your eyes. BO 3X. Be swallowed by the whale. BO 3X. See, sense, feel, know, and live your transformation in the belly of this leviathan. Breathe out and open your eyes.

5.* Close your eyes. BO 3X. See, live, and feel Jonah leaving the belly of the whale on the third day. Experience this emergence. Breathe out and open your eyes.

6. Close your eyes. BO 3X. Be Jonah on the hillside crying at the destruction of the gourd. Hear God telling him that he is forgiven for not having learned his lesson in the whale, and teaching him, by the analogy of the gourd, compassion for the human existence. Breathe out and open your eyes.

7. Close your eyes. BO 3X. See and know why we cannot escape our "destiny," and why the messages from invisible reality must be heeded, and why we must be obedient to the great unseen. Breathe out and open your eyes.

* * *

JOB

INTENTION: To be centered and balanced. To become patient.

FREQUENCY: Once a year at the same time and date for 30 seconds.

1. Close your eyes. BO 3X. Live, as Job, the bet made between God and Satan, that you can be turned from faith in the certainty of the reality of God. Breathe out and open your eyes.

2. Close your eyes. BO 1X. Know and live your loss, as Job, not understanding why, but staying in the moment, accepting and responding. Don't accept to remain sad. Breathe out and open your eyes.

3. Close your eyes. BO 3X. See and sense yourself resisting the suggestions of the false comforters who have come to visit you seemingly as friends. Don't become self-blaming, or critical of God. BO 1X. Know, now, who and what is a true friend. Breathe out and open your eyes.

4. Close your eyes. BO 3X. Hear the still small voice issuing forth out of the whirlwind confirming your faith in God. Hear what this voice has to tell you. What do you see now? Breathe out and open your eyes.

5. Close your eyes. BO 3X. See and know, as Job, that you understand what Moses experienced at the burning bush. Breathe out and open your eyes.

6. Close your eyes. BO 3X. See, feel, and sense all that you have lost being restored to you. BO 1X. Know why the physical disease has not disappeared. Breathe out and open your eyes.

7. Close your eyes. BO 2X. Feel, as Satan, the loss of God's realm, having fallen from there. BO 3X. Know and live why God has to retrieve Satan as a reason for the creation of the world. Breathe out and open your eyes.

* * *

NAOMI AND RUTH

INTENTION: To know loyalty.

FREQUENCY: Once a year at the same time and date for 30 seconds.

1. Close your eyes. BO 3X. Sense and feel yourself as Naomi, accepting of the stranger and caring for everyone equally. Breathe out and open your eyes.

2. Close your eyes. BO 3X. Be the wise woman, giving counsel to each of your close family members in the measure necessary for each. Breathe out and open your eyes.

3. Close your eyes. BO 3X. Shout, at the top of your lungs silently, the phrase "Whither thou goest I shall go." Hear the reverberation of this exclamation. What does this effort tell you about yourself? Breathe out and open your eyes.

4. Close your eyes. BO 3X. Feel, as Ruth, the yearning for God and be willing to follow your teacher without question. See and sense yourself allowing change, plunging into the new, accepting the freedom in the moment. Breathe out and open your eyes.

5. Close your eyes. BO 3X. Go into the field of wheat having given up your worldly attachments. Gather the leavings of the harvest left by Boaz, the great master of prayer. Know

what this work has brought to you. Breathe out and open your eyes.

6. Close your eyes. BO 3X. Feel the strength of Boaz. BO 1X. Feel, sense, and know how prayer gives eternal strength that gives eternal life. BO 3X. Lie at the feet of Naomi and Ruth and never die. Breathe out and open your eyes.

* * *

ESTHER

INTENTION: To know truth.

FREQUENCY: Once a year at the same time and date for 30 seconds.

l. Close your eyes. BO 3X. Live as King Xerxes, being taken in by physical beauty. BO 2X. Live how this beauty disconnected from truth brings destruction to the beholder and to the bearer. Breathe out and open your eyes.

2. Close your eyes. BO 3X. Be Esther, the one who is beautiful but not yet living in truth. BO 1X. Know that we always have the opportunity to fulfill that inner beauty which is truth. Breathe out and open your eyes.

3. Close your eyes. BO 3X. See and feel yourself as Mordecai, a teacher of truth, having to save your people from extermination. BO 3X. Know and understand how truth is linked to acknowledging your identity and identification with God. Breathe out and open your eyes.

4. Close your eyes. BO 3X. Listen to the truth you are hearing. BO 1X. Being Esther, reveal your truth to save the community. BO 1X. See all the evil Hamans of the world receive

their punishment, measure for measure, and how this punishment may redeem them. Breathe out and open your eyes.

5. Close your eyes. BO 3X. Know how giving credit to your sources brings satisfaction to you and to the larger community. Breathe out and open your eyes.

6. Close your eyes. BO 3X. See, sense, and know how the armies of evil have to be actively engaged and destroyed. Know the lesson evil learns in this active encounter. Breathe out and open your eyes.

7. Close your eyes. BO 3X. Feel and live the peace and harmony created in the world by Esther's bravery and courage to reveal the truth. Know how her faith in the Almighty brings reward to herself and the greater community. BO 1X. Be King Xerxes enjoying the benefits of the revelation of Esther. Breathe out and open your eyes.

8. Close your eyes. BO 3X. Live, as Mordecai, egoless and claiming no personal glory for Esther's meritorious action. Sense and feel and value of ordinary life. Breathe out and open your eyes.

* * *

DANIEL

INTENTION: To become disciplined.

FREQUENCY: Once a year at the same time and date for 30 seconds.

1. Close your eyes. BO 3X. Live, as Daniel, the prophetic way of independence and detachment from the ordinary affairs of daily life. Breathe out and open your eyes.

2. Close your eyes. BO 3X. See, live, and know how God sustains life when we live as simply as Daniel.
BO 1X. Eat simply.
BO 1X. Dress simply.
BO 1X. Be simple in spirit.
What happens?
Breathe out and open your eyes.

3. Close your eyes. BO 3X. See, sense, feel, and know as Daniel the difference between dreams and visions. Breathe out and open your eyes.

4.* Close your eyes. BO 3X. See, like Daniel, each of the countries of the time as animals eating each other.
BO 1X. See Babylonia as a lion full of pride. Sense this will to power.
BO 1X. See Nebuchadnezzar, the king of kings, as full of greed, wanting to destroy the Jewish people in Persia for seventy years to have their riches and richness. Sense how his imperialism wants more and more.
BO 1X. See him as a panther stalking and conquering country after country to impose his ideology.

5. Close your eyes. BO 3X. Know, like Daniel, how will, discipline, and faith in God bring the protection of God in the face of all adversity. Breathe out and open your eyes.

CHAPTER SIX

FINAL WORDS

It is said in spiritual life that if five percent of the world's population were to undergo a shift in consciousness, the entire population would undergo a return to Eden. By climbing our own ladder of self-mastery, we can form a new "holy nation" and become "light(s) unto the nations." Then, Isaiah's prophetic vision is fulfilled: swords are beaten into plowshares, nations shall not lift up sword against nation, we shall learn war no more (Isa. 2:4), and the leopard shall lie with the kid, wolf with the lamb, lion with the calf (Isa. 11:6).

To become a light unto the nations is the highest spiritual attainment for Western Monotheism. It has three parts: 1) the end of evil; 2) the literal defeat of death; and 3) union with God.

Originally the symbol of Monotheism was the menorah, or seven-branched candlestick, branching from one main stem and made from one piece of precious metal. The menorah represented the Tree of Life, the eternal light of the Divine entering the world; the inner structure of humanity as divine light; as well as the physical structure of the vascular and central nervous systems of the human body.

If we retrieve the sparks of holiness and let them shine through us, we shall become bodies of light sending the sparks upwards. In return for recapturing this light, we become enlightened from above through what is called "*shefa,*" divine grace, the heavenly light flowing into us. Eventually we become light-bearing beings, developing thereby a new physiology, biology, emotionality, mentality. The new transformation we call the "resurrective body," one that knows no death to become the eternal, perfect, absolutely free being we were at birth.

Monotheism regards the defeat of death as a *literal* reality. It will be accomplished on earth at the time of the "end of days." This is a time of judgment where it will be determined who will merit eternal life in a world of love, which has replaced the world ruled by the will to power. In this "day," linear time comes to an end. We shall be living in the presence of the present in alignment with God, in the existence of no time. This day is called "Resurrection."

For those believing in resurrection there isn't a sense of nor need for circular time embodied in reincarnation and immortality of the soul. These latter two elements are intimately intertwined and are rather late additions to monotheistic spiritual wisdom. They came into prominence with the influence of Greek civilization and the advent of the Jewish kings.

With individuality comes its natural outgrowths: immortality of the individual soul and individual reincarnation. This is not to say that the resurrectionists did not subscribe to some form of reincarnation. They did, but only within the family line. This was consonant with the ancient emphasis on purity and the maintenance of purity through bloodlines. In keeping with the necessity of purity, it made burial rituals and burial sites very important. With regard to the latter, it was necessary for family members to be buried in a designated family plot so that there would not be a mixing of foreign elements, which was significant for future reincarnation, and particularly important for resurrection where the bones of the entire family would be restored to life, all the members being together again. As well, for the time of resurrection they understood that when the accounting and weighing of each person's soul took place at the end of days, to determine whether eternal life will be granted, how the commandments had been carried out, would be assessed.

Once a being dies, his/her bones remain in place in the earth and at the end of days when the judgment is rendered from on high as to who receives the grace and benediction for eternal life, then the flesh of that being is restored to the bones. Hence, the prohibition in Judaism against cremation. The bones have to be available to be restored to life.

As evidence for the restoration of flesh to bones, we have only to look at Ezekiel 37:

> The hand of the Lord was upon me, and the Lord carried me out in a spirit, and set me down in the midst of the valley, and it was full of bones; and He caused me to pass by them round about, and, behold, there were very many in the open valley; and, lo, they were very dry. And He said unto me, "Son of man, can these bones live?" And I answered: "O Lord GOD, Thou knowest." Then He said unto me: "Prophesy over these bones, and say unto them: O ye dry bones, hear the word of the LORD: Thus saith the Lord GOD unto these bones: Behold, I will cause breath to enter into you, and ye shall live. And I will lay sinews upon you, and will bring up flesh upon you, and cover you with skin, and put breath in you, and ye shall live; and ye shall know that I am the Lord. So I prophesied as I was commanded; and as I prophesied, there was a noise, and behold a commotion, and the bones came together, bone to its bone. And I beheld, and lo, there were sinews upon them, and flesh came up, and skin covered them above; but there was no breath in them. Then said He unto me: "Prophesy unto the breath, prophesy son of man, and say to the breath: Thus saith the Lord GOD: Come from the four winds, O breath, and breathe upon these slain, that they may live." So I prophesied as He commanded me, and the breath came into them, and they lived, and stood up upon their feet, an exceeding great host. Then He said unto me: "Son of man, these bones are the whole house of Israel; behold, they say: Our bones are dried up, and our hope is lost; we are clean cut off. Therefore, prophesy, and say unto them: Thus saith the Lord GOD: Behold I will open your

172 CLIMBING JACOB'S LADDER

graves. O my people; and I will bring you into the land of
Israel. And ye shall know that I am the Lord, when I have
opened your graves, and caused you to come up out of
your graves, O my people. And I will put My spirit in
you and ye shall live; and I will place you in your own
land; and ye shall know that I the Lord have spoken, and
performed it, saith the Lord. (Ezekiel 37:1-14)

We have then the immortalists reaching toward the
Divine to transcend the coils of the perceived earthly enslavement, and the resurrectionists bringing the Divine down to
this earth to turn the darkness of enslavement into the light of
freedom.

Up to now the resurrectionists and the immortalists
within the Monotheistic tradition have managed to live side
by side, with actually the immortalists having more adherents
in these times, particularly with the influence of Eastern traditions having gained sway over the Western mindset.

Monotheistic tradition is devoted to the creation, procreation, and continuous perpetuation of life. For the
ancients, life was passed on by way of clearly spelled out
means of transmission, keeping God squarely in the center of
all activity. It was only possible to truly live by making life
attune to God's prescription for living endlessly and eternally. Life not lived according to divine prescription was essentially meaningless and self-indulgent, servicing that force
wanting to end life on this earth.

Someone asked me recently if living forever might not be
extraordinarily painful. You could find yourself isolated, seeing as how everyone around you may die, given that not
everyone has reached that state, and you would be in a world
where you didn't know anybody, the argument continued. I
responded by saying that in becoming the immortal selves we
are meant to be, in that consciousness we would not be
thinking about, nor experience death nor the pain of loss.

Our world becomes apperceived in an entirely independent way. We focus on, think about, and experience only life. In the immortal world of God where there is no death or loss, we don't know it, and there is no pain.

This book is written in the service of the force of life to help clear up the moral ignorance that has brought this planet to a dangerous precipice of incalculable damage as we come to the close of the sixth millennium. The third millennium of the common era shall bring a great awakening to the dangers brought us by the field of technology and science, which has spawned much idolatry. It has coaxed people into worshipping machines, and uses these machines to hypnotize us. We are kept asleep, while we are being made into a rapidly illiterate society. This technological age has also pushed us into further depleting our natural resources, posing another threat to our survival.

We are currently absent a spiritual foundation in the West. We seem to be seeking for one in the midst of the avalanche of technological change swirling around us that seems to overwhelm and leave us unanchored if we are not quick-witted enough to figure it out in the mini-bytes of time allotted to us to absorb the disinformation streaming at us daily through the media. Paradoxically this social climate provides the perfect soil for the planting of the seeds of Spirit that may help to take us out of the morass of suffering and dehumanization plaguing us in a degree that is staggering. It is when suffering is greatest that the yearning for Spirit becomes most intense.

My contribution is to bring to light a spiritual wisdom of the West as a remedy to the ever-increasing pollution and destruction of our mind, body, and environment. It is then the keys to freedom, consisting of the Bible, Ten Commandments, and Three Vows, become the way from the enslavement of everyday life to the attainment of spiritual freedom.

The question before us is whether we can wake up in

time to save ourselves and go through the necessary cleansing and purification that is required to turn this deteriorating planet into the Eden that is its potential. I believe this book is a contribution in that direction; it is offered as an attempt to awaken our consciousness by remembering God.

When we remember ourselves on all levels of existence, truly attach our memory intellectually, emotionally, physically to Divine memory, where Spirit remembers us, then we have the conditions set for eternal and everlasting Life. The defeat of death is accomplished, and we have fulfilled our purpose for existing here as heroes of God, having restored light out of darkness, our cosmic mission, for which our reward is irrevocable freedom.

NOTES

[1] I added murderers. Rumi confined his observations to thieves and drunkards.

[2] Karma is understood as the cosmic law of cause and effect, meaning that for every action we undertake, mental or physical, there is a consequence that we must receive and experience that will be exactly proportionate to the action taken.

[3] Esau has a ruddy complexion, meaning he is short-tempered by nature.

[4] Valentin Tomberg, in his monumental work *Meditations on the Tarot* (New York: Penguin Books), describes these functions brilliantly in his discourse on the 14th Major Arcanum = Temperance.

[5] Dreams, in Western spirituality, have always been recognized as a real existence and as an entirely revelatory experience. It is as valid an existence as waking life and does inform our waking existence. I explore this point in greater depth in the story of Joseph, the "father" of dream reading in Western life.

[6] This theme is repeated in the story of Daniel and King Nebuchadnezzar.

[7] For those already in the grip of chronic pain and not able to find relief, it is not easy to reflect on one's contribution to its presence. I think this reflective process can only really start after the pain has quieted. To this end I would recommend using my book *Healing Visualizations* (Bantam, 1989).

About the Author

Dr. Gerald Epstein is uniquely qualified to write this book. After receiving his M.D. in 1961, psychiatric certification in 1965, and psychoanalytic certification in 1972, he worked as a practicing psychiatrist and psychoanalyst for nine years. In 1974, he met his teacher, Colette Aboulker-Muscat, and became an initiate of the Kabbalah of Light, a spiritual Monotheistic tradition at the root of the major religious doctrines of Judaism, Christianity, and Islam. In 1974, he also began his study of the techniques of healing through imagery. Over the last twenty-five years, Dr. Epstein has become the leading exponent, practitioner, and teacher in this field in the United States. He has published books, articles, and research on this subject. His books *Healing Visualizations* and *Waking Dream Therapy* are standard reference works in this field. His *Healing Into Immortality* (Bantam, 1994; ACMI Press, 1997) provides the most comprehensive foundation in print for understanding the spiritual medicine of the West. He has appeared on national TV, radio, at major conferences, and internationally. He lives with his wife and two children in New York City where he teaches and practices this work.